*For my daughter, Mallory Claire Fairman,
in the hopes that she will say it
less and understand it more.*

FUCK

WITHDRAWN

Word Taboo and Protecting Our First Amendment Liberties

CHRISTOPHER M. FAIRMAN

1/10

SPHINX® PUBLISHING
AN IMPRINT OF SOURCEBOOKS, INC.®
NAPERVILLE, ILLINOIS
www.SphinxLegal.com

Published by Sphinx Publishing, an imprint of Sourcebooks, Inc.
P.O. Box 4410, Naperville, Illinois 60567-4410
(630) 961-3900
Fax: (630) 961-2168
www.sourcebooks.com

Library of Congress Cataloging-in-Publication Data

Fairman, Christopher M.
  Fuck : word taboo and protecting our First Amendment liberties / Christopher
M. Fairman.
    p. cm.
  Includes bibliographical references and index.
  1. Obscenity (Law)—United States. 2. Freedom of speech—United States. 3.
Fuck (The English word) 4. Taboo, Linguistic. I. Title.
  KF9444.F35 2009
  342.7308'53—dc22
                                    2009016762

Printed and bound in the United States of America.
VP 10 9 8 7 6 5 4 3 2 1

Contents

Prologue

This is a book about the word *fuck* and its intersection with the law and the concept of taboo. In the first chapter, "Why *Fuck*?" I explain why I didn't sanitize the title. I applaud my publisher and editors for supporting this decision.

Because of this title, my book will likely be the target of many a giggle from middle schoolers. Some parents may shield their kids' eyes. Those same youthful eyes could just as easily end up reading this book under the covers by flashlight—drawn to it by the very taboo that makes *fuck* a dirty word.

I know that feeling. It was 1971 when my parents brought home David Reuben's bestseller, *Everything You Always Wanted to Know About Sex* (But Were Afraid to Ask)*. It was not so hidden in the bottom of my parents' nightstand on the right side. I used to sneak it out, read it under the covers or in the bathroom, then sneak it back into place. I got lax on one of those trips to the bathroom and stashed it under the sink… and then forgot about it. Later, when Mom was cleaning, she found it. That night at dinner, she revealed her alarming discovery. Looking straight at my big brother Mark, she let the table know that she found the book and had returned it to its proper place and whoever had taken it should stop. Big brother had all he could stand of the accusatory glare and said, "It wasn't me, ask Chris."

The shock brought the whole subtle reprimand to a halt. I was not quite eleven, so Mark's "not me" defense was no guarantee of exoneration. I could have shifted blame back on him with a simple lie. Instead, I didn't look up from my fried chicken. My silence was my confession.

The memory of that dinnertime inquisition didn't resurface until I was writing this book. At eleven, I remember I had no difficulty digesting the chapters of my curiosity. I'm confident I would be a more informed reader today, but this taboo primer on sex did me no harm in 1971. Yet little did I know that my preteen encounter with taboo would have such a latent impact.

After the sex book incident, I continued to have this strange attraction to the forbidden. I wanted to know what was going on in all those places where I wasn't supposed to be: topless bars, nude beaches, dirty book stores, X-rated movie theaters, peep show arcades, punk rock music clubs, gay clubs, the afterhours. I wasn't willing to blindly take anyone's word about what was good or bad or right or wrong without seeing for myself. Part journalist, part tourist, and always nervous, I grew up on my own quest to experience what you might call the "seedy underbelly" of American culture. Now I can look back and appreciate that this common theme of attraction and repulsion was due to taboo.

Just as Dr. Reuben talked frankly about sex, one of our strongest taboos in both language and act, these pages contain frank discussion of our most taboo word. *Fuck*. Reuben got a generation talking about sex topics like cunnilingus, the Three-Headed Turtle, and shoe fetishes.

He demystified what people do. I'm interested in what we say or won't say—word and language taboos. And I want you to think about the word *fuck*.

A brief note about the limits of this project: I'm interested solely in the word *fuck*, its variations, and why this particular four-letter word has such a robust intersection with the law. While I find interesting the scholarly work of those who strive to understand the power relationships expressed by "who fucks" and "who gets fucked," this article doesn't address that issue of language usage.[1]

Similarly, those interested in other offensive words, such as *nigger*, may see some parallels, but I've deliberately not tried to fashion an ambitious understanding of all offensive and hurtful speech.[2] I'm not even trying to corner the four-letter word market. *Shit*'s happened.[3] I leave *cunt* for another day. Rather, I have tried to keep my *fuck* focus.

This book is based upon an earlier law journal article I wrote, entitled simply "Fuck," that was published by *Cardozo Law Review* in 2007. My experiences with that article illustrate many of my themes in this book. I was a little naïve when I completed the article. Surely, I thought, my audience—a curious mix of legal academics and the second-year law students who populate the newly selected editorial boards of law journals—wouldn't have a problem with this topic. I was wrong.

I made my first wave of submissions of "Fuck" to law journals in March 2006. I mailed a hard copy of the piece to the attention of the lead articles editor (or someone of similar title) at the top thirty law reviews. Articles editors—those second-year law students I spoke of—read the piece and decide if it's right for their volume. After submission, you wait weeks, sometimes months, for a publication decision. Not in my case. Five days after I started the process, the rejection letters started to arrive. The first ding came from *Harvard Law Review*:

> Dear Professor Fairman:
>
> We have read with interest your manuscript, entitled "F**k." We have completed our review process and have decided not to make an offer to publish your manuscript. Thank you for your interest in the *Harvard Law Review*.[4]

I wanted to reply:

> Dear Editors of the *Harvard Law Review*:
>   Thank you for your rejection letter. However, there must be some confusion. I did not submit a manuscript entitled "F**k" to you. I did submit an article entitled "Fuck." In my article, I make the point that it is silly to use euphemism for a word that every one knows, especially when your use is to quote someone else's use. Out of curiosity, what does this other article "F**k" say on the subject?

Who knew the editors of the *Harvard Law Review* were so affected by taboo? Of the other fifty journals that had the chance to publish the article, only one other resorted to euphemism. The *Kentucky Law Journal* had the subject line of its rejection letter as "Article Submission 'F—k'."[5] At least Harvard got the number of letters right.

Even more curious to me is why the "Editors of the *Harvard Law Review*" would send me an essentially anonymous per curiam rejection, yet they've published the word *fuck* thirty-two times before my submission and once afterward in their own articles.[6] (Brace yourself. This paradox of using the word while simultaneously rejecting the word is a common theme surrounding taboo.)

The prevalence of word taboo in the twenty-first century is startling. The fact that this book exists and is in your hands is due to taboo. Another submission anecdote makes this point. After the consistent rejections from my first wave of submissions, I prepared a second wave. To expedite submission of the next batch, I chose only journals that would take electronic submissions. With my list of twenty or so new possibilities, I sat down at my computer during lunch and was ready to go.

Tuesday, April 11, 2006, 11:38 a.m., I emailed a copy to the *University of Kansas Law Review*. As I pressed the send button, I thought, "As a Kansan by birth, maybe the journal will recognize a native son and help me out." And maybe it did, but not how I expected.

Tuesday, April 11, 2006, 12:03 p.m., twenty-five minutes after submission, I heard the chime of incoming email. I checked. It was a rejection letter from the *Kansas Law Review*:

> Thank you for submitting your article to the *Kansas Law Review*. We are unable to extend an offer for publication.
>
> > Sincerely,
> > David Hague, Managing Editor
> > *Kansas Law Review*[7]

Now I deal with rejection pretty well, but this one sent me reeling. It came so quickly that I was still sitting at my computer submitting to other journals when the rejection poured in. *Kansas Law Review* prides itself on being prompt, but this was ridiculous. You couldn't have read the article in twenty-five minutes. They saw one thing—the title—and decided to pass. That's how powerful this one word is.

The *Kansas Law Review* rejection is not without irony. Although they haven't made as robust use of the word as *Harvard* has, *Kansas* has twice printed articles containing *fuck*. The first use of *fuck* was in Professor Camille Hébert's article "Sexual Harassment is Gender Harassment" in 1995. Camille Hébert is, by the way, a colleague of mine at Ohio State.[8] She is also an alumnus of the University of Kansas Law School. The second use was in a recent piece by University of Kansas Law Professor Stephen McAllister titled "Funeral Picketing Laws and Free Speech."[9] Apparently *fuck* is acceptable when it comes out of the mouth of one of their own.

Still, I saw the humor of this instant rejection, so the next day I shared the story with Professor Brian Leiter. Leiter runs a blog, Brian Leiter's Law School Reports, a respected source for basically law school gossip—who's on the move, who's taking their place, what is the faculty at Blank Law School squabbling about, who hired the best cadre of new law teachers. And each spring, what's going on with the law review submission process. As I predicted, Leiter used my tip for an entry in his blog the following day:

World's Fastest Article Rejection by a Law Review
One of our alums in law teaching, Christopher Fairman (Ohio State), reports that the *Kansas Law Review*, which prides itself on promptness, rejected

> this article of his only twenty-five minutes after he submitted it! It seems they read the title. Who knew the Kansans were so sensitive?[10]

The phrase "this article of his" was actually a link to a draft of the "Fuck" article that I had posted in the bepress Legal Repository, the Berkeley Electronic Press collection of law articles. It was April 13, 2006. In the days and weeks that followed, I learned much about the power of the web and of taboo.

Leiter dropped a single pebble into the Internet pond. It caused ripples at first, followed by waves. A handful of other law blogs thought it was funny and picked up on it.[11] The readership of these blogs started downloading the bepress draft by the hundreds, then thousands. On April 14, 2006, one day after Leiter's blurb, three days after its rejection by *Kansas*, "Fuck" was number one on the bepress list of "The 10 Most Popular Articles."[12] Let me put this in perspective. I posted the article on bepress on March 23, 2006. On April 3, 2006, it had only six downloads—one of which was mine. One month later, on May 2, 2006, it had 5,610 downloads, but not a single offer to publish it.[13]

After the working paper was already perched at number one on the bepress most popular list, I got a call from a bepress spokesman. He had a request on behalf of the publisher: Would I mind if they altered the title of my article to read 'F*CK'?

I answered: "Would I mind? Of course I would mind! Did you read the first chapter, first paragraph for that matter, where I denounce self-censorship and use of euphemism?" I continued, "And if you intend to censor the title against my wishes, please let me know now so I can be sure to bring it up in the press interview I'm headed to." No changes were ever made to the title.

What would motivate an e-publisher to want to alter the title of his own "bestseller," so to speak? Word taboo. The taboo associated with *fuck* is so strong that it clouds rational decision-making. Even though thousands of unoffended readers were downloading copies of "Fuck," the publisher had doubts about the propriety of using the word. The solution? Let's stick an asterisk in the title! It's as if that tiny six-pointed punctuation mark inoculates the word. If the bepress bigwigs want to practice this linguistic nonsense, that's one thing. But this was an attempt to impose their view on me—illustrating how easy it is for individual effects of word taboo to quickly become institutionalized.

This type of self-censoring continues even now. In a recent article by Professor Dan Subotnik in the *Southern California Review of Law and Social Justice*, he cites me for the proposition that "copulation is a hot topic in academic circles [a]s evidenced by the reaction to an article by Ohio State law professor Christopher M. Fairman... Within two months of publication, the article had been downloaded at least 18,000 times." What article was cited? "Christopher M. Fairman, "F ___," 28 *Cardozo L. Rev.* 1711 (2007)."[14] Another quick electronic search reveals that the same journal published the word *fuck* seven times previously.[15] If you are looking for consistency in the jurisprudence of *fuck*, there's none, so it's best to settle into the duality right now.

Concern about the title of "Fuck" is only one of many complex ways that insidious word taboo infects us. Notice that Leiter's initial post never mentions the title of the article. The other men who linked to Leiter's blog followed the same practice. Consciously or subconsciously, by choosing not to use the title of the article to talk about the article, these bloggers reinforce the very taboo they poke fun at Kansas Law Review for following. Ann Bartow at the Feminist Law Professors Blog called them out on their sanitized postings:

> "Fuck" the Law Review Article
>
> Yes, "Fuck" is the title as well as topic of this article by Prof. Christopher M. Fairman of Ohio State's Moritz College of Law. I'm not too demure to blog it, unlike shrinking violets Brian Leiter and Michael Froomkin (or maybe they just want to avoid the porn spam that is sure to follow?). Via Feminist Law Prof. Susan Franck, who noted that she "read the introduction of the piece itself (not just the abstract) and it's a really interesting one... Particularly how the genesis of the piece got started (i.e., students being uncomfortable with courts writing graphically about women in sex discrimination cases)."[16]

Professor Bartow's insight is that we should focus on the word *fuck* and its influence, not merely on the rejection anecdote as Leiter does. Bartow also models how we can unwrap our words from the bindings of taboo. *Simply use the word when that's the word to use.*

Like Bartow, tax law Professor Paul Caron is another blogger who doesn't give in to taboo. His TaxProf Blog is lauded as a must-read in the legal community and general blogosphere. April 15, 2006—"Tax Day" no less—Caron posted "Fairman on 'Fuck'" and included the abstract of a second draft that I posted on SSRN, the Social Science Research Network.[17] The SSRN, like bepress, is an eLibrary of hundreds of thousands of abstracts and full texts of social science scholarship. The exposure generated by Caron's high profile post exposed my work to a vastly broader audience. What had been contained to law professor blogdom now went mainstream.

Exposure to a broader, popular audience certainly reinforced my sense that there are a lot of people in the world who are interested in learning more about this four-letter word. This can all be monitored through SSRN download statistics. In 2007 over 80,000 authors uploaded more than 158,000 papers and abstracts to SSRN's eLibrary. Users then downloaded almost sixteen million full text documents, or about one hundred downloads per article. Looking only at the top 1,500 law authors, the 1,500th law author averaged eighty-four all-time downloads per article; the average new downloads per new paper is only thirty.[18] I posted "Fuck" on SSRN in mid-April

2006. In one month it had 487 full-text downloads—more downloads than any of the other five articles I have posted to SSRN. By mid-June, the download count was almost ten times greater at 3,986. As summer ended and a new academic year began, August 16, 2006, the download count was 6,288. By September 27, 2006, "Fuck" became the number one most downloaded article in virtually every annual top ten list the SSRN compiles; it jettisoned me to the spot of top author for a year. Each month the "Fuck" article continued to gain in downloads, and as of February 20, 2009, the total number of downloads on SSRN was 24,147 and over 332,557 had viewed the abstract of the article; an additional 12,622 downloads were on bepress.[19] By any measure, "Fuck" the article was hugely popular based on the number of downloads.

But what do downloads of a law review article really mean? Both SSRN and bepress have a common goal of rapid dissemination of new scholarship. Can download data also serve as a quality indicator of individual works, authors, or law schools? I think the number of downloads means just that—how many people have downloaded, pure and simple. You can imagine my surprise when I discovered that according to some, my downloads don't count. In March 2007, Brian Leiter, the blogger, introduced for the first time a new faculty ranking—the "Most Downloaded Law Faculties, 2006."[20] While Leiter claims that the data reports the fifteen most downloaded schools during all of 2006, there was a curious omission. According to Leiter:

It was necessary to exclude Ohio State [ranked 10th] and Emory [ranked 8th] whose presence in the top 15 was due entirely to one provocatively titled article by Christopher Fairman, who teaches at Ohio State and is visiting at Emory; without Fairman's paper, neither Ohio State nor Emory would be close to the top 15.

Why was this exclusion necessary? Leiter states that it's the "provocative title." Yet other law journal articles have had provocative titles. Harvard Law Professor Randall Kennedy's best-selling book is titled *Nigger*.[21] Before Professor Kennedy completed his book, he previously published an article on the same topic, "'Nigger!' as a Problem in the Law," in the *University of Illinois Law Review*.[22] If it had been a recent post, would Leiter have censored it, too? What triggers exclusion? Is he using George Carlin's list of seven words you couldn't say (in a law review title)?[23] Or is this like obscenity was to Justice Stewart—Leiter just knows it when he sees it.[24] What if I had sanitized the title to "F-Word"? Would my downloads count now?

The exclusion reminds me of pop star Britney Spears's controversial new song, "If U Seek Amy."[25] The Parents Television Council—self-appointed speech police—are outraged because when Britney sings the lyric it sounds like "f-u-c-k me." While the PTC lobbied the Federal Communications Commission to ban the broadcast as indecency, the song sold 107,000 digital copies in the United

States to debut at Number 92 on the Billboard Pop 100.[26] But if you think like Leiter, Billboard should exclude the song from its rankings altogether. After all, it's "necessary" since the huge number of sales was undoubtedly due to the provocative title.

Leiter's rankings are, however, "Leiter's Law School Rankings." He is free to report, fine-tune, include, exclude, or manipulate the numbers as he wishes. But what led to the choices he made? This is another example of word taboo that forms the thesis of this book. The word taboo against *fuck* grips the subconscious and often overpowers the ability of some to calmly and rationally react. It can also compel some individuals to impose their language standards on others.

Acquiescence to people trying to censor our words ultimately costs us in the currency of language—our ideas. I learned this firsthand with the "Fuck" article. Why was the article punished for its popularity? From what I can tell, the thinking was this: Legal academics, the "right people," thousands of them, downloaded the articles of Brian Leiter and the rest of the academic community who offered their thoughts to the downloading public. It was a common horde that downloaded "Fuck." They saw a dirty word and clicked away, unknowingly inflating the download count.

Yet anyone who has ever used SSRN knows that its two-step download process corrects for this type of single-click phenomenon.[27] People downloaded my article for the same reason that they downloaded any piece: they're interested in it. It is just that maybe the "they" doing the downloading is different. I fear that there's some type of undemocratic intellectual snobbery at play here.

The truth is that I don't know who's downloaded my articles any more than anyone else does. I do know that, as a direct result of posting my article, I've received suggestions from law professors, linguists, lawyers, and librarians from the United States, Canada, Great Britain, Germany, Croatia, Australia, and China. I've heard from students with an interest in the subject at all levels: law, graduate, undergraduate, and high school. Having taught for seventeen years (nine as a high school history teacher and now eight in law schools), a special treat for me has been the many former students who have sent me their comments. I have emails from judges and journalists, and from wrestlers and weirdoes, too—each giving me their own two cents on the subject. I don't, however, see this type of diversity of audience as a negative.

I decided to follow the life of the mind with the hope that someone would read what I painstakingly pecked out with two fingers on my keyboard. I'm grateful to everyone who has used their valuable time to read the article and now this book. It's my response to those who criticize my pandering to a popular, voyeuristic mass. It hasn't been my ambition to become *Der Jäger des F-Worts*—Hunter of the F-Word—as a German news magazine labeled me, or even better, "Professor Fuck," as another reporter did.[28] But if I must don the four scarlet letters so that my daughter retains the right to tell the government to "leave me the fuck alone," I will.

Christopher M. Fairman
Columbus, Ohio
February 20, 2009

CHAPTER ONE

Why *Fuck*?

Oh fuck. Let's just get this out of the way. You'll find no f-word, f*ck, f--k, @$!%, or other sanitized version used here. This is quite a change from Professor Allen Walker Read's 1934 scholarly treatment of the word, "An Obscenity Symbol"—fifteen pages and eighty-two footnotes penned without once printing the word *fuck* anywhere in the article.[29] I won't even cleanse my title as Dr. Leo Stone did with his landmark piece, "On the Principal Obscene Word of the English Language."[30] And why should I? This isn't the first time you've seen the word and, if you keep reading, it certainly won't be the last.

Let me explain the genesis of this book. A trilogy of events motivated me to start this project. The first occurred during my second year as a law professor. I was teaching a course in Professional Responsibility, and the lesson for the day was attorney racist and sexist behavior. The case I assigned from a leading casebook was liberally sprinkled with *fuck, cunt, shit, bitch,* and the like.[31] Sensitive to the power of language, I recited the facts myself rather than ask a student, as was my norm. After the course was over, I was reviewing my student evaluations and discovered this: "I was a little disturbed by the way he seemed to delight in saying 'cunt' and 'fucking bitch' during class. I think if you're going to say things like that in class, you should expect it to show up on the evaluation." Now I was the one a little disturbed.

How could any educated adult, much less a graduate student in a professional program, be offended by hearing these words read from a court opinion? I decided then that someday I wanted to explore this topic in more depth. However, early in my career and armed with other safe, doctrinal projects on my research agenda, this one had to wait.

The idea of writing a book about *fuck* resurfaced a year later when I read about the plight of Timothy Boomer. While canoeing on the Rifle River in Michigan, Boomer fell overboard, letting forth a "fuck" or two. As if his day wasn't bad enough, a nearby deputy sheriff gave him a ticket—and not for unsafe canoeing. Instead, he was cited for violating an 1897 statute that proscribed: "Any person who shall use any indecent, immoral, obscene, vulgar, or insulting language in the presence or hearing of any woman or child shall be guilty of a misdemeanor."[32] Then Boomer was convicted and sentenced in municipal court to a $75 fine and four days of community service or three days in jail for cursing within earshot of women and children. Amazed by the fact that Boomer was convicted at all, I was unprepared for what happened next. The conviction was upheld on appeal to the district court. Flabbergasted that this could happen in the twenty-first century, my curiosity about the legal implications of *fuck* was piqued. (As for Boomer, wiser minds prevailed in his second appeal in which the Michigan Court of Appeals reversed his conviction.)[33]

While my background research was ongoing, a third event crystallized my intention to write this book. United States District Court Judge Algenon Marbley was reported as sending federal marshals to arrest a man, Robert Dalton, for contempt of court. The offense was sending the judge an email calling Judge Marbley a "fuck-up." Now I can understand contempt charges if this happened in open court, or if the man had been a lawyer involved in the case. However, the facts recounted by the newspaper implicated none of these reasons. It was a private email sent from Dalton to Judge Marbley criticizing his handling of the settlement of a consumer class action lawsuit. Dalton was not even a member of the plaintiff class. His only connection was that he was a longtime critic of the local car dealer who was the defendant in the class action.

This scenario is a far cry from pornographer Larry Flynt's outburst before the United States Supreme Court during oral argument in *Keeton v. Hustler Magazine, Inc.*[34] Flynt shouted, "Fuck this Court! You're nothing but eight assholes and a token cunt."[35] Chief Justice Warren Burger arrested Flynt for contempt of court. Now the Chief's reaction could be justified as maintaining order in the courtroom and preventing interference with judicial business; Flynt could have screamed anything that day and been subject to arrest. Not so in Judge Marbley's case.

I don't profess to be a constitutional scholar, but I always thought the heart of the First Amendment was the right to criticize the government—federal judges included. In my mind, Dalton should have been able to yell "fuck the judge" at the top of his lungs from his rooftop if he wanted to. While Judge Marbley ultimately withdrew the contempt charge, it's clear that he was solely concerned with the actual use of language. After Dalton was dragged into court, Judge Marbley scolded him saying, "As an articulate man, you could have found another way to express yourself." Only after Dalton conceded that "in retrospect, I could have used other creative words to express the strong sentiment I have," did the judge withdraw the contempt charge.[36]

Judge Marbley's reaction can't be explained as Midwestern sensitivity either. Historically, Ohio judges haven't had such a severe reaction to *fuck*. In 1970, amidst the usual Ohio State–Michigan football frenzy, someone printed bumper stickers that said "Fuck Michigan." A law student put one on his windshield and was arrested by the Columbus Police Department for violating the city's obscene-literature law. Judge James A. Pearson dismissed the case, concluding that it would be absurd to interpret the sticker to mean "have sexual intercourse with the state of Michigan." He further concluded that most of the citizens of central Ohio would feel that the bumper sticker had some redeeming value.[37] So what led to such a different reaction by Judge Marbley to the same word decades later in the same Midwestern city in what is surely a much more tolerant generation?

These legally trained minds—a law student, a law enforcement officer, a state district court judge, even a federal judge—each heard the word *fuck* and suddenly lost the ability to calmly, objectively, and rationally react. If *fuck* has power over these people, what are the limits of its influence? After these incidents, I knew this book had to be written—after I was tenured.

Now I want to be clear: No one at the College of Law or The Ohio State University has ever, in any way, tried to limit my academic freedom. Instead, I've experienced exactly the opposite; the faculty and administration have generously supported my research efforts. Still, the thought of writing this book made me skittish. I wasn't prepared to embark down *fuck*'s path until I had the protection of academic freedom that tenure provides. I could see with clarity the overreactions by others to the word *fuck*. But when it came to myself, I didn't recognize my own behavior as a form of self-censoring. The subconscious force of taboo that ultimately becomes central to my thesis is part of me, too.

POWER OF TABOO

Three consonants and a vowel ordered one way—"f-c-u-k"
—is the acronym and trademark of fashion company French
Connection United Kingdom, a multimillion-dollar designer
label coveted by many worldwide. With the slightest of
alterations, this corporate trademark becomes "f-u-c-k"—a
word so forceful that its utterance can land you in jail.
What transforms these four letters into an expletive of such
resounding power?

To fully understand the legal power of the word, I draw
upon the research of etymologists, linguists, lexicographers,
psycholinguists, and other social scientists. Collectively, their
research offers an explanation for the visceral reaction to
fuck: word taboo.

In every culture, there are things that we're not supposed
to do and things we're not supposed to say: taboo acts and
taboo words. In Western society, many of these taboos relate
to sex. *Fuck* is one of these taboo words. Its taboo status is
likely due to our deep, subconscious, negative feelings about
sex. As Edward Saragin put it: "In the entire language of
proscribed words, from slang to profanity, from the mildly
unclean to the utterly obscene, including terms relating to
concealed parts of the body, to excretion and excrement as
well as to sexuality, one word reigns supreme, unchallenged
in its preeminence."[38] *Fuck.*

Forged in our subconscious, word taboo compels many to
engage in self-censoring. Some people are so affected by taboo

that it becomes a word fetish. These individuals are not content to refrain from using the word themselves. Rather, these speech vigilantes want to restrict your vocabulary as well. The silence of the majority empowers this small segment of the population to try to sanitize our words under the guise of reflecting a greater community. When they capture the ear of our politicians or policemen, taboo is institutionalized through law.

The law of *fuck* is inconsistent, confusing, and contradictory. From the vantage point of constitutional doctrine, poor Tim Boomer aside, use of the word itself isn't obscene given the development of the law of obscenity. Indeed, the First Amendment accommodates vulgar *fuck* when core political speech is involved. The Supreme Court said I can even parade through a courthouse with a jacket emblazoned with "Fuck the Draft" for all to see.

But if the lead singer of the band U2, Bono, accepts a Golden Globe award exclaiming "this is really, really fucking brilliant," or Cher or Nicole Richie says *fuck* just once on live TV, the Federal Communication Commission is poised to sanction the broadcasting stations for the fleeting reference as indecent speech describing sexual activity. If that conclusion isn't baffling enough, those same TV stations can show Tom Hanks swearing like a soldier on the beaches of Normandy in *Saving Private Ryan* and that's fine. Such is the confusion surrounding the law and *fuck*.

The legal implications of the use of *fuck* reveal both inconsistencies in its treatment and tension with other identifiable legal rights that the law simply doesn't answer. We may live under a Bill of Rights that exclaims Congress "shall make no law" abridging the freedom of speech, but that doesn't stop the law from targeting the word *fuck*. Taboo is the tool that helps me understand why the law acts and reacts to the word as it does.

FUCK ≠ SEX

Fuck is all about sex and nothing about sex all at the same time. Virtually none of the uses of the word that I discuss have anything to do with sex. Timothy Boomer's "fuck!," "Fuck the Draft," Bono's "fucking brilliant," the ever-present "fuck you"—none of these are sexual in meaning. So why do we choose that word? The subconscious mind and its universe of instincts and inherited memories grafts powerful, dark, sexual meaning to the word *fuck*. When a speaker experiences intense excitement and simultaneously reaches into his vocabulary pool, the powerful word that's grabbed may derive its strength from taboo. Despite the denotation intended, the taboo remains imbedded like linguistic genetic code. Whether the listener understands the speaker's intended meaning or not, word taboo engrafts the negative connotation and hence its inherent power.

Reaction then depends upon audience. When the hammer misses its mark and lands on your thumb, the "fuck" your buddy hears is the one you meant. The same is likely true if you whisper in your partner's ear that you want to fuck him or her. The reaction, of course, depends upon how well you understand your partner, but there was no confusion on your meaning. Simply put: Words have meanings. If we can distinguish between different meanings of *fuck*, why can't our government?

The failure of the law to consistently distinguish between sexual and nonsexual uses of *fuck* is much of the problem. Even if you accept the idea that it's okay for the government to restrict access to truly obscene material—that is, patently offensive descriptions of sexual conduct appealing to the prurient interest—the litmus test is that the material is about sex. Most of the time, *fuck* isn't. It's creepy to think about Uncle Sam peering under my sheets, but it's flat out wrong to allow him to dictate false meanings to the words I choose. When the FCC declares all uses of *fuck* are per se sexual and indecent, taboo triumphs over reason. The same marginalization of speech occurs when the law, under the influence of taboo, encourages private employers and public schools to restrict workplace and school speech.

If we want to diminish the taboo effect, silence isn't the solution. Neither is punishing the use of offensive language. Such attempts to curtail the use of *fuck* are doomed to fail. Fundamentally, *fuck* persists because it is taboo, not in spite of it. We must recognize that words like *fuck* have a legitimate place in our daily life.

Whether you shout it in the street or whisper it in the bedroom, say it deliberately as a political protest or accidentally let it slip out, make a single fleeting reference or sing an expletive-laden rant, intend to be funny or downright foul, if you say "fuck," someone wants to silence you. We shouldn't passively watch as tiny coalitions with a webpage and a word fetish take some of our words away. When it's the government trying to cleanse your language, you should really worry. We shouldn't tolerate any part of our representative government mucking around in our words: we elect senators, not censors.

At issue isn't just protection for some entertainer's potty mouth. Words are ideas. If the government can control the words we say, it can also control what we think. Ultimately, my concern is for the preservation of our most basic liberty—a freedom of the mind.

UNDERSTANDING *FUCK*

In order to protect this liberty, we must first understand why the law's treatment of *fuck* puts that freedom at risk. How can a single four-letter word foreshadow such doom? The next chapters of this book arm you with the essential background and analytical tools you need for this inquiry. Chapter 2 explores the modern usage of *fuck*. It seems like it's everywhere these days. But don't let ubiquitous *fuck* confuse you. Just because everyone says it doesn't mean that everyone accepts it. This seeming paradox comes from the power of taboo. Chapter 3 presents taboo as the essential concept for understanding the force of this four-letter word. Chapter 4 explores the etymology of *fuck*, providing a valuable historical account of both usage and taboo. When the contributions of linguistics and psycholinguistics are added in chapter 5, a complete picture of taboo's impact emerges. *Fuck* carries with it layers of unhealthy subconscious sexual fears. An extreme emotional reaction produces word fetish examined in chapter 6. The effect of taboo manifests in self-censorship and, if left unchecked, institutionalized taboo. Chapter 7 concludes with a survey of the law's inconsistent treatment of *fuck*, an inconsistency caused by taboo.

The remainder of this book explore the nuances of this jurisprudential mess. There is a chapter that tackles each of the separate constitutional doctrines that's been applied to *fuck* by the Supreme Court: fighting words, obscenity, vulgarity, and indecency. I also explore the FCC's regulation of speech and the role taboo plays in its policymaking. The last chapters highlight *fuck* and the law of the workplace and schools, where taboo also leads to a chilling of speech by workers, students, and teachers. The final chapter tackles the future of *fuck* and predicts its continued resilience.

Before predictions about *fuck*'s future or tales of its past, the next chapter looks at the current use of *fuck* and the love/hate relationship we have with this four-letter word.

CHAPTER TWO

Ubiquitous *Fuck*

Suffice it to say, *fuck* is everywhere. One recent Internet search revealed that *fuck* "is a more commonly used word than mom, baseball, hot dogs, apple pie, and Chevrolet."[39] It's present in movies, television programs,[40] and popular music.[41] Former President George W. Bush reportedly used it with aplomb. (His Vice President Cheney, too.) Yet, *fuck* remains a word "known by all and recognized by none."[42] We live with this dichotomy: *fuck* is ubiquitous and used by most of us, but its public utterance still generates controversy.

THE PARADOX

Author Patty Campbell describes her experience researching why the use of dirty words in young adult literature was increasing, but there was narrower tolerance for them. After her initial research turned up dry holes, she Googled the "Big

Daddy of swear words"—*fuck*. "A testament to the power of that word is the way the search made me feel paranoid and perverted—as if I might end up on a government list somewhere."[43] Campbell isn't immune from what she calls the "Pottymouth Paradox." We are all attracted to "our worst word" and at the same time recoil from its use. This combination fuels its popularity.

An Associated Press poll conducted in 2006 found that nearly three-quarters of Americans questioned said they encounter people using profanity in public frequently or occasionally, and two-thirds said they think people swear more than they did twenty years ago.[44] What makes this survey interesting is the fact that it was conducted without using any of the allegedly profane words it was trying to measure. (The poll did ask specifically about the "f-word," however.) Twenty-seven percent of those polled reported using *fuck* a few times a week or more, and another 37 percent used *fuck* a few times a month or more. This yields 64 percent using *fuck*. Then there is the 35 percent who claim they never use it. (One percent is not sure—now what the fuck is that about?)

How useful is this AP poll? Linguist Benjamin Zimmer thinks it's riddled with flaws.[45] First, he notes that self-reported evaluations of speech patterns are inherently unreliable, and especially so when the questioners don't even refer to the words they are asking about in the survey. This failure to identify the words that constitute "profanity" or "swear words" leaves the entire categorization up to the judgment of the respondents. Additionally, questions about whether people swear more now than twenty years ago are particularly susceptible to "recency illusion," the belief that things you have noticed only recently are in fact recent. At least the questions about *fuck* contained some level of specificity—even if by euphemism.

A better methodology is to examine oral frequency of use of taboo words. In a 1969 study of conversations overheard in natural settings, foul language was used in 12.7 percent of adult leisure conversations, 8.1 percent of college conversations, and 3.5 percent of on-the-job conversations, signifying that taboo speech is used more often in casual conversation than in more formal situations.[46] A more recent oral frequency study confirms these levels. Swearing accounts for 3 percent of on-the-job talk and 13 percent of leisure conversation.[47]

Other studies on the frequency of swearing focus on which particular words are used most frequently. For example, *fuck* is among the seventy-five words most often verbalized.[48] The first field study of offensive speech was conducted by Timothy Jay and presented in his 1992 book, *Cursing in America*. Jay reports that *fuck* is by far the most frequently used taboo word by both men and women. His research also confirms that men swear more than women.[49]

Yet another form of research in this area is to test for the level of offensiveness of words. One British study recently ranked taboo words, not by the frequency of use but by offensiveness. *Fuck* came in third place behind *motherfucker* (second) and *cunt* (first).[50] But remember, that's British cursing. The Brits also ranked *wanker* in fourth place, *bollocks* eighth, *arsehole* ninth, and *shit* comes in a distant seventeenth. Given these results, I am unwilling to retreat from the belief that *fuck* remains the Queen Mother of dirty words in the United States. Whatever the limitations on the research of frequency of taboo words, we can still safely conclude that the use of *fuck* is widespread. It permeates our entire culture.

FUCK IN PRINT

Although it's hard to believe, *fuck* was barely tolerable in print until the 1960s. The saga to preserve access to D.H. Lawrence's classic, *Lady Chatterley's Lover*—a novel banned on three continents—illustrates this point.[51] The book was originally published in Florence in 1928. Because of D.H. Lawrence's use of *fuck*, it was banned as obscene in the United Kingdom until 1960, when publisher Penguin Books won an obscenity trial. In Australia, not only was the book banned but even a book describing the British obscenity trial was banned. In the United States, Grove Press, Inc. of New York published the book in 1959. After confiscation by the U.S. Post Office, the publisher successfully challenged the order and the Second Circuit held that the work was not obscene.

Conceding that "so-called four-letter words" appear in a portion of the book, the Second Circuit found those passages "subordinate, but highly useful, elements to the author's central purpose."[52] The court concluded:

And should a mature and sophisticated reading public be kept in blinders because a government official thinks reading certain words of power and literary value is not good for it? We agree with the court below in believing and holding that definitions of obscenity consistent with modern intellectual standards and morals neither require nor permit such a restriction.[53]

Today, book banning based upon the word *fuck* is unthinkable. Authors can draw upon all of our words, taboo or not, for expression. That is precisely what Allan Sherman has done. In one of the cleverest uses of *fuck* in print, Sherman's book, *Rape of the A.P.E.*,[54] includes chapter 2, titled "Short Chapter, Long Footnote." The chapter contains a single word—"Fuck." It is then followed by a nine-page, single-spaced footnote that discusses our fear of the word and how it has impacted our attitudes about sex. Included in the footnote is the author's own anecdote of how he freed himself from the bondage of the word by forcing himself to type *fuck* over and over. Five hundred pages later, he was immune to the taboo. Using this technique, Sherman graphically demonstrates just how much baggage we force *fuck* to carry.

Now just because book banning is a thing of the past in this country doesn't mean the print media has exorcised all its demons. Newspapers and magazines still engage in much hand wringing whenever *fuck* is newsworthy. For example, in

June 2004, former Vice President Dick Cheney told Senator Patrick Leahy to "fuck yourself" during a heated exchange on the Senate floor.[55] Now that's real news. *The Washington Post* reported the exact use of the phrase. In contrast, *The Washington Times* avoided the word altogether by reporting that Cheney "urg[ed] Mr. Leahy... to perform a sex act that's anatomically impossible."[56] And so it goes. Some papers won't print *fuck* at all, while others use asterisks. Journalist Suzanne Moore points out the silliness of the asterisk strategy: "When a reader reads f*****g, I should imagine that he or she knows what it f*****g means."[57] Papers that refuse to use *fuck* or insist on a euphemism reflect a form of self-censoring based on word taboo.

Let's not forget, *fuck* printed in a newspaper can still raise quite a ruckus, as it did in Fort Collins, Colorado, in September 2007. The editor of the Colorado State University newspaper, the *Rocky Mountain Collegian*, published an editorial that said simply in large type, "Taser this. Fuck Bush."[58] This sparked a heated dialogue between CSU students, alumni, local members of the Fort Collins community, and students from other schools about whether or not the decision to print the editorial in a school-affiliated paper, or in any paper for that matter, was acceptable. Despite pressure to resign, editor-in-chief J. David McSwane refused to voluntarily step down. The Board of Student Communications ultimately admonished him for violating the student media code, but he remained editor-in-chief.[59]

FUCK IN FILMS

Fuck may not be the word of journalism, but it plays a starring role in movies and films. The use of *fuck* in R-rated movies intended for adult audiences is common. It found exceptional use in *Scarface* (Universal Pictures 1983), *Blue Velvet* (Metro Goldwin Meyer 1986), and *Pulp Fiction* (Miramax 1994). The use of *fuck* is not limited to the dark side of cinema either. Hugh Grant repeatedly uttered "fuck" in the comedy *Four Weddings and a Funeral* (Gramercy Pictures 1994).

One of the more interesting recent uses of *fuck* comes in Mel Gibson's *Apocalypto* (Touchstone Pictures 2006). This film shows the decline of Mayan civilization in the sixteenth century. After one of the tribesmen is bitten by a poisonous snake, Middle Eye, one of the principal characters says simply, "He's fucked."[60] The use of *fuck* is highlighted because the film uses subtitles for the Mayan dialogue. Gibson's incorporation of *fuck* into the dialogue of sixteenth-century indigenous people, and a nonsexual use to boot, is consistent with some etymological accounts.

The most important film using *fuck* is also about *fuck*. On November 10, 2006, producer/director Steve Anderson released his documentary, *Fuck* (Mudflap Films 2006).[61] The film examines the impact of the word *fuck* on our culture through interviews, film and television clips, music, and original animation. Anderson describes the difficulty inherent in producing a film where its very title is subject to a negative reaction:

All along I've wanted to call the movie just simply *Fuck*, because that is what the film is about. It's the center of the film. But just like the word itself, there's been much debate about what reaction the title would get. It's obvious that you couldn't print the ads for a film entitled *Fuck* in newspapers like the *LA Times* or *New York Times*. Some newspapers like *LA Weekly* might print it. How does it go on a marquee at a festival? So my feeling is this: The title of the movie is *Fuck*. We'll make a design with an asterisk or a symbol, but the distributors or whoever takes the film, they'll have their own ideas. They might use an asterisk. They might use two asterisks. They might rename it for their purposes just like they do in the newspapers. But when you go to the theater and you see it onscreen, or when you see it on DVD, the name of the movie will be *Fuck*. So in an odd way that's what the movie is all about: people's reaction to this word, the reaction to the title. The debate we've had as filmmakers has reflected society's debate about the word itself. Is it appropriate? Can we get away with it? Is it a good thing? Is it a bad thing? I think the discussion over the title of the film reflects exactly what the film is about, so I decided to stick with that.[62]

Anderson got his title, but he also got the marketing difficulties he had predicted as theaters posted all kinds of euphemisms for the title, including "The Four-Letter Word Film."

WHAT THE FUCK?

From films to fashion, *fuck* has presence. It's a jacket with the word on it that generates *fuck*'s greatest legal victory in *Cohen v. California*. Today, an entire fashion empire is built on *fuck*, or should I say FCUK. The provocative logo FCUK is the acronym and trademark of fashion company French Connection United Kingdom.[63] Founded in 1969, French Connection began using the distinctive logo in 1997, which immediately resulted in an 81 percent spike in profits. The company began exploiting the similarity with *fuck* by printing T-shirts with messages like: "hot as fcuk," "cool as fcuk," "fcuk me," "fcuk fear," "too busy to fcuk," "lucky fcuk," and "fcuk this." In October 2005, the company announced plans to reduce the use of the fcuk logo, as profits dropped an estimated 69 percent to £5.1 million GBP, from £16.2 million GBP in 2004. Nonetheless, one million FCUK T-shirts have been sold.[64]

CELEBRITY SLIPS

It's not the T-shirts, though, that galvanizes national attention. It's the fuck-ups—those little gaffes made by people in the public eye—that fascinate us. In October 2006, Barbra Streisand was performing a number of sold-out shows at Madison Square Garden. A heckler wouldn't be quiet. When Streisand finally had enough she fired off: "Shut the fuck up! Shut up if you can't take a joke." This was national news, reported by Fox ("Shut the (expletive) up!"), *USA Today* ("Shut the (expletive) up!"), and the *New York Post* ("Shut the f--- up."), to name a few.[65]

The same media attention ensued after Diane Keaton's *fuck* slip. On January 15, 2008, the veteran actress was being interviewed on *Good Morning America* by Diane Sawyer. During an inspired riff in which Keaton coveted Sawyer's ripe, pillowy lips, the iconic screen personality lamented how scoring such good fortune would have allowed her the luxury of not having "to work on my fucking personality." The Internet blogs were ablaze in references, usually without using the word but linking to a video clip so you could hear it yourself. I must admit, there is something remarkable about seeing a seasoned actress and veteran journalist, both impeccably dressed and cheerful, and then hearing how naturally "fucking" slipped into the conversation.[66]

Juxtapose the Keaton incident with Anthony Hopkins's second appearance on the critically acclaimed *Inside the Actor's Studio* hosted by James Lipton.[67] Lipton asks each guest on his show a series of ten questions. One of the ten is, "What is your favorite curse word?" When Lipton asks Hopkins the question, Hopkins immediately responded, "fuck." He embellished, "A Jesuit priest said to me once, you know what the shortest prayer in the world is? I'm fucked." It seems that Hopkins's affinity for *fuck* is shared by others in his field. Jack Lemmon responded to the same question with "cocksucking motherfucker." Comedian Dave Chappelle prefers simply "fuck." [68]

The use of *fuck* seems even more natural coming from the mouths of our leaders. Former Vice President Dick Cheney's "go fuck yourself" comment to Senator Leahy is classic. The "Curser in Chief," former President George W. Bush, was not to be outdone.[69] During a visit from Prime Minister Tony Blair, Bush said into a live mike that Syria needed "to get Hezbollah to stop doing this shit." There's also Bush's pre-Iraq war comment, "Fuck Saddam, we're taking him out." This administration was supposed to set a new moral standard—and they have. The Second Circuit described these incidents as support for striking down the latest FCC policy on *fuck*.[70]

PARADOX REVISITED

Everywhere you look, Campbell's "Pottymouth Paradox" pops up. Research shows that most Americans routinely use *fuck*, but it's still our most offensive word. We'll wear its near equivalent on our clothes and enjoy it in our movies. Read it in our books; read about it in our newspapers. And of course, watch our favorite entertainers and politicians make the expected slips of the tongue. When you say *fuck*, or hear it, or read it, your subconscious sits like a devil on your shoulder poking you with his pitchfork and hissing, "That's a dirty word, a really dirty word, a really dirty word about sex." Taboo.

In the next chapter, we explore taboo and its power over us all.

CHAPTER THREE

The Power of Taboo

Central to an understanding of the legal implications of the word *fuck* is that the law doesn't provide a complete answer. Ultimately, it's the concept of taboo that provides guidance. But as you will discover, our study of taboo is often stymied by taboo. In other words, taboo speech is so taboo that it hasn't been regarded as a legitimate topic for scholarship. Saying *fuck* is a cultural taboo; studying *fuck* is a scholarly taboo. Dr. Leo Stone's lamentation in 1954 that "scholarly information about this important word is remarkable for its scarcity"[71] remains true today—more than half a century later.

My own experience reflects this notion of scholarly taboo. At the start of this project, several of my own colleagues counseled against it. They thought either I would never be able to get this book published (and certainly not with this title), or if I did, it would be so offensive that no one would read it. But there was always a subtext: that it would be a waste of my scholarly energy to pursue this subject. It was as if research on dirty words was, in itself, somehow dirty. Such is the power of taboo.

I'm also well aware of the risk of offending some readers. But isn't this really my duty? As Sanford Levinson, my legal ethics professor at the University of Texas School of Law, explained, "Teachers in particular may be guilty of evading part of their own responsibilities if they become too fastidious in 'avoiding... words that shock.'" Discussing offensive speech requires that one be willing to breach standard norms and run the "risk of offending. I think it is as simple as that."[72] I can't agree more.

Despite the pressures to forgo study in this area, an interdisciplinary approach to *fuck* and the law is possible. Many different disciplines contribute to an understanding of *fuck*. Etymologists provide us with a valuable historical account of usage and taboo. Lexicographers demonstrate how the conscious efforts of those who compiled dictionaries deliberately purged the word for centuries. Sociologists note the cultural influences on offensive speech. Linguists expose the sexual and nonsexual meanings of *fuck*. Psycholinguists build on this knowledge to show the tremendous influence our subconscious mind has on the use of *fuck*. Still other social scientists search for an integrated theory to explain *fuck*.[73] At the center of all these explanations for *fuck*'s treatment lies a common denominator—taboo.

ORIGINS OF TABOO

The English word *taboo* comes from the Tongan word *tabu*. In the 1770s, Captain James Cook explored the Pacific islands and observed the behavior of the Polynesian people. In their journals, Captain Cook and fellow shipmates recorded *taboo* as a significant local word meaning forbidden, such as when a thing was not to be eaten, entered, or touched.[74] Likely due to this origin, taboo is a trait often associated with so-called primitive cultures. This is a mistake. Taboo exists in primitive societies and western contemporary ones alike.

Taboo is a proscription on behavior for a specific community in a specific context. In every culture, there are both taboo acts (things that you're not supposed to do) and taboo words (things that you're not supposed to say). While some taboo acts have corresponding taboo words, others don't. In their book *Bad Language*, Lars Andersson and Peter Trudgill offer a useful comparison. Consider our taboos relating to sex and cannibalism. Sex isn't entirely forbidden; it's regulated by a set of conscious and subconscious rules. Given the appropriate time, place, and person, sex is not taboo. Incest, however, is taboo— so is the word *motherfucker*. Cannibalism is another one of our taboo acts. However, there are no unspeakable, unprintable English words—taboo words—referring to cannibalism.[75] And although incest and cannibalism may be taboo to us now, no taboo is absolute and universal. Egyptian Pharaoh Ramses II married several of his daughters; the survivors of the 1972 Andes plane crash ate the dead to stay alive.[76]

Even though there are no absolutes, there are typical categories of taboo. Taboo associated with food gathering and preparation is common. Body effluvia—feces, urine, menstrual fluid, snot, and semen—are often subject to taboo. Sex organs and sex acts are also frequently taboo targets. Similarly, taboos about death, disease, and dangerous animals occur often. Sacred beings, objects, and places also are associated with taboo. What do these categories have in common?

Collectively, they all deal with situations in which one is at risk of serious harm. Improper handling of food can lead to sickness and death. Our body fluids not only harbor disease but can also contaminate others. Dangerous animals and disease directly threaten our health and security. One even puts the soul at risk when dealing with the sacred. Thus, specific behaviors viewed as dangerous to the individual or community become taboo to protect the community from harm.

FROM TABOO ACTS TO TABOO WORDS

But I'm concerned with taboo words, not acts. I can wrap my mind around cleanliness taboos such as avoiding contact with bodily fluids, don't play with your feces, etc. But how does this transform into a taboo against saying *shit*? It's as if Prohibition in the 1920s forbade not just the sale of alcohol but saying the word *whiskey* as well. So how do we move from taboo behavior to taboo words?

The transmutation has a scientific explanation. Let me use effluvia taboos as an illustration. Researchers in public heath and hygiene, like Valerie Curtis, contend that our hygiene instincts are the product of disgust.[77] Curtis found that while people have difficulty explaining their reactions, they nonetheless have a powerful feeling of disgust to avoid filthy, sticky, oozing, teeming matter. Seeing a disgust trigger (like vomit or pus) automatically produces a subconscious hygienic reaction. Disgust helps us avoid those things that were associated with the risk of disease in our evolutionary past.

The disgust reaction would obviously be strongest if confronted with eating or touching effluvia. Seeing body fluids, or images of them, also invokes disgust. But even thinking about our excretions (and the body parts that are responsible for them) generates disgust. Because the disgust reaction is involuntary, hearing the words triggers the response. Consequently, the words themselves become the objects of disgust and, therefore, taboo. In this way, taboo acts (handling feces) transform into taboo words (saying *shit*).

A similar process occurs in the other categories of taboo. The fear of harm is so strong that the subconscious reacts not only to the object of fear but also to the very thoughts of encountering the object of fear. Because thoughts are words, the words become taboo. So a dangerous animal can be taboo, as well as the name of the taboo beast. The word for *bear* used by our Germanic ancestors is unknown today because it was never recorded. The word *bear* itself means "the brown one" and is a euphemism for the unknown word. Similarly, in parts of West Africa, the word for *snake* is taboo.

Like the bear, the reptile is referred to euphemistically as a stick or piece of rope.[78]

An additional reason for not using the names of dangerous animals is a fear that the animal might hear its name and attack. For example, certain fishermen in Papua New Guinea avoid talking about sharks and stingrays for fear of inviting an attack. If they are seen, the fishermen call them *woo* or fish instead of the more specific *bawang* (shark) or *beoto* (ray). This word *taboo* is also reflected by a Ukranian proverb: "One speaks of the wolf and it runs into the house." Precisely the same type of word taboo is reflected by the English proverb, "Speak of the devil and he comes running."[79] Just as some refrain from saying the devil, others avoid speaking the name of their deity. Due to its sacred nature, the Hebrews would not say their word for God.[80] To make it harder to blaspheme, the name was written without vowels (YHVH).

SACRED OR DISGUSTING?

Taboo words relating to sex are also commonplace—which leads us back to *fuck*. Sigmund Freud points out that *taboo* can reflect two meanings: one that is "sacred or consecrated" and the other "impure, prohibited, dangerous, and disgusting."[81] Nobody really knows whether *fuck* is taboo because it falls into the category of "sacred and consecrated" or "prohibited and disgusting." In fact, there's a lot about the word we don't know. But by following the work of a handful of researchers from various disciplines including etymologists, lexicographers, linguists, psycholinguists, and biomedical researchers, we can develop a more complete understanding of why the word *fuck* is taboo. In the next chapter, we start with the work of those who study the history of words— etymologists.

CHAPTER FOUR

Fuck Etymology

To better understand our word of the day, let's consider its origins. Where did *fuck* come from? Answering this is no simple task. Our understanding of taboo language is hindered by taboo itself. Early lexicographers under the influence of the cultural taboo excluded the word from their dictionaries. In turn, modern efforts to piece together the origins of *fuck* are hampered because of its deliberate exclusion from these earlier authorities. In the absence of authoritative information, speculation fills the void. Conflicting origins abound. Erroneous etymologies persist. Simply put, *fuck*'s history is in dispute.

HISTORICAL LEXICOGRAPHY

Let's start with the first recorded use. The quest for the earliest written record of *fuck* is an example of historical lexicography. Historical lexicography is the study of the etymology, chronology, and meaning of words that traces the meaning of the word back to its earliest appearance in print.[82] All later developments in the word's usage are then illustrated by dated and documented quotations using the word. This process has inherent limitations. One reason that the word *fuck* is so hard to trace is that it was used far more extensively in common speech than in easily traceable written forms. Using this historical method, lexicographers conclude that even the first recorded use of *fuck* is in dispute.

Some sources point to the poem "Flen flyys"—a Latin and English mix satirizing the Carmelite friars of Cambridge composed before 1500.[83] The poem is named from the first line, "Flen, flyys, and freris," or "fleas, flies, and friars." The line containing *fuck* is: "Non sunt in coeli, quia gxddbov xxkxzt pg ifmk." The Latin phrase "Non sunt in coeli, quia," means "they are not in heaven, since." Then the encoded phrase "gxddbov xxkxzt pg ifmk" is translated by substituting the preceding letter in the alphabet, while being mindful that i was then used for both i and j, v was used for both u and v, and vv was used for w. In the end, this leaves "fvccant vvivys of heli." The translated line reads: "They are not in heaven because they fuck the wives of Ely."[84]

Based upon this early source, some conclude that *fuck* was considered shocking from the first and the use of code was because of its unacceptability.[85] Another possible explanation is that the phrase was coded because it accused some church folks of serious misbehaving. As with so much of *fuck*'s history, it's uncertain to what extent the word was considered acceptable at the time.

Others claim the first written use of *fuck* is in a Scottish poem by William Dunbar, "In Secreit Place," in 1503.[86] The stanza including *fuck* is:

He clappit fast, he kist, he chukkit
As with the glaikkis he wer ourgane—
Yit be his feiris he wald haif fukkit:
Ye brek my hairt, my bony ane.[87]

Appearing in the works of this major Scottish poet and aristocrat also casts doubt on the term being unacceptable from the first. Any squabble over whether the poet or the friars came first can't compare to the muddled etymology.

Simply put, the etymology of *fuck* is unclear. Some etymologists trace *fuck* to Germanic languages with an original meaning "to knock" and cognates such as Old Dutch *ficken*, Middle High German *vicken*, and German *ficken*.[88] This widely accepted derivation, however, has its critics. According to Dr. Leo Stone, the general trends of vowel sound change in English fail to account for the evolution of *ficken* to *fuck*.[89]

Professor Allen Walker Read believed that *fuck* came from Latin cognates like *pungo* (to prick) and *pugil* (boxer), which comes from the root *pug-* (to thrust).[90] Stone is also skeptical of this etymology and that Read's "strong opinion about a unilateral etymology is stated somewhat arbitrarily, without documentation of intermediate sources."[91]

Germanic origin is also seen from an Indo-European etymology.[92] The sound of *p* in ancient Indo-European came to be pronounced *f* by Germanic tribes as in Greek *pod* with English *foot*. The Indo-European *g* became pronounced *k* as in Greek *gonu* and English *knee*. Thus the Indo-European *pug* becomes *fuck*.

Another possible etymology is through the French *foutre* and Latin *futuere*,[93] but there are similar doubts and an absence of lineage for this derivation as well.[94] Stephen Skinner's 1671 *Etymologicon Linguæ Anglicanæ* is targeted as introducing etymological confusion with derivation through the French *foutre* ultimately to Greek.[95] Possibly there is a hybrid derivation in which *foutre* participated with *ficken* to produce *fuck*.[96] Still other etymologies suggest Old Norse *fukja*, "to drive," which gives us *windfucker* and *fucksail*.[97] Or how about *firk*, a common English word from the eleventh to the seventeenth century meaning a sharp, sudden blow. One scholar suggests that out of the natural looseness of coarse speech, we simply dropped the *r*.[98]

Of particular interest to the lawyer-lexicographer is the suggestion of an Egyptian root *petcha* (to copulate).[99] Dr. Reinhold Aman, publisher of *Maledicta* and a copious researcher of offensive words, uncovered the following gem. During the 23rd Egyptian Dynasty, many legal documents were reinforced with the following tripartite curse: As for him who shall disregard it, "May you get fucked by a donkey! May your wife get fucked by a donkey! May your child fuck your wife!" The hieroglyph for the legal curse—containing five large erect penises—makes the message clear.[100]

What then do you make of all these possibilities? Each putative etymology has flaws. It's impossible to definitely identify the precise origin of *fuck*. Although some scholars embrace etymologies outside of the Germanic range, they are likely outliers; most etymologists would characterize *fuck* as likely Germanic, even though we can't pinpoint exactly the word from which it came down.

LEXICOGRAPHY'S LASTING SHAME

Understanding the etymology of *fuck* is hampered by its exclusion from our dictionaries. *Fuck* made its lexicographic debut in John Florio's 1598 Italian-English dictionary, which included *fucke* in the definition of *fottere* along with *jape*, *sard*, *swive*, and *occupy*.[101] There's no consensus if *fuck* was ever acceptable or precisely when it became considered offensive. But from 1795 to 1965, the word did not appear in any widely read English dictionary.[102]

The exclusion of *fuck* from the leading dictionaries illustrates a deliberate attempt to cleanse the language of this word. The purge emerges by the late seventeenth century and becomes well entrenched by the eighteenth century.[103] By the late eighteenth century most dictionaries were being produced for use in schools; *fuck* was excluded over concerns of corrupting young minds.[104]

Not surprisingly, when Samuel Johnson, Jr. published the first American dictionary in 1798, he omitted *fuck* in order to inspire modesty, delicacy, and chastity of language. Noah Webster's crusade against vulgar words sealed *fuck*'s fate in America: exclusion from his dictionaries of 1806, 1807, 1817, 1828, and 1841. This Websterian tradition was carried back across the Atlantic when in 1898 the authoritative *Oxford English Dictionary* (OED) deliberately excluded *fuck*. On this matter, Read is particularly critical and calls it a "lasting shame" that the editors would not be true to the scientific spirit of the project and "offset the remissness" of the earlier lexicographers.[105] Indeed, its first appearance in the OED was not until 1972 where the entry gives the guarded "ulterior etymology unknown."[106]

In case you're wondering when *fuck* made it into print in the United States, you guessed it, there are conflicting accounts. Jesse Sheidlower recounts that the earliest openly printed use of *fuck* in the United States was in 1926.[107] Fred Shapiro beats that by a wide margin. He discovered a published 1846 case from the Supreme Court of Missouri stating, "The slanderous charge was carnal knowledge of a mare, and the word 'fuck' was used to convey the imputation."[108] Shapiro also notes the 1889 use of "motherf——g" by the Texas Court of Appeals and the 1897 use of "motherfucking" by the Texas Court of Criminal Appeals.[109]

ETYMOLOGIES

Although I can't offer certainty on the etymological question, I can alert you to several urban-legend false etymologies that *fuck* derives from acronyms.[110] The two most common acronymic phrases are "For Unlawful Carnal Knowledge" and "Fornication Under Consent of the King." There are dozens of permutations as well.[111] None of these acronyms, however, explain *fuck*'s origin.[112] Words that are acronymic—created by taking the first letter of the words in a phrase—are a purely twentieth-century development. More specifically, none of the *fuck* acronyms was ever heard until the 1960s.[113] Moreover, *fuck* has been in use far too long to allow these supposed origins to be possible.

Closer scrutiny of "Fornication Under Consent of the King" proves it's a false etymology. Under this acronym, couples wishing to have sex had to first get a royal permission slip and post it for all to read. A moment's rational thought should tell you that if the King were in charge of handing out such documentation, he would have little time for anything else. Additionally, the word *fornication* precludes such an explanation. Fornication relates to premarital or extramarital sex. By definition, it does not apply to married couples, thereby nullifying the fornication permit idea. An alternative explanation of the acronym, that conquering troops had orders to rape the conquered, also lacks foundation. There is no evidence of such a royal proclamation.

The second acronym, "For Unlawful Carnal Knowledge," was supposedly used to identify adulterers, rapists, child molesters, and other perverts. As part of their punishment, they were forced to wear a sign around their necks while serving their sentence in the stocks. The weak link in this linguistic chain is the three-letter word *for*. Although the use of public shaming was a popular punishment in the seventeenth and eighteenth centuries, any signage announcing the crime would have been succinct. If the crime was stealing a loaf of bread, the prisoner's sign would read "Thief" or "Stealing," not "For Stealing Bread." The "For" would always be superfluous.

Why do these popular urban-legend etymologies persist? One suggestion is that like all acronymic explanations, we're attracted to a "hidden knowledge" factor. We all like to think that we each have some tidbit of information that others don't.[114] Or maybe the acronyms reinforce a preconception that a dirty word like *fuck* must have a dark story of origin— one full of stockades, rapists, or royal fornication permits. The unglamorous truth is that *fuck* trickled into the English language just like the rest of our vocabulary. It came from another language. Spelled differently for sure. Probably pronounced differently as well. Over time, the word became our *fuck*.

FUCK'S RESILIENCE

Whatever its origins, *fuck*'s longevity in English is surprising given the condemnation and concerted efforts to stamp out its use, which continued throughout the twentieth century. *Fuck*'s continued vitality is even more amazing when compared to the fate of its sixteenth-century synonyms. Recall the earliest dictionary entry for *fuck* listed it along with *jape*, *sard*, *swive*, and *occupy*. Ever heard of *jape* or *sard*? They are virtually unknown. Chaucer's *swive* is considered archaic. And *occupy* returns to English, but with a nonsexual meaning.[115] Why then is *fuck* so resilient? As we'll explore in the next chapter, linguistics and psycholinguistics provide some answers.

CHAPTER FIVE

Linguistics, Psycholinguistics, and Taboo

Both etymologists and lexicographers advance our understanding of *fuck*, yet fall short of providing an explanation for the emotional power of the word. To unlock these secrets, we must turn to linguistics (the scientific study of language) and even more so to psycholinguistics (the study of the psychological factors that affect language). What is exposed is the gripping influence of cultural taboo to reach through the centuries and control your behavior today.

WHAT'S JAPE?

Let's start with key insights from linguistics. Remember John Florio's sixteenth-century Italian-English dictionary and his short list of *fuck* synonyms: *jape*, *sard*, *swive*, and *occupy*? One question that puzzles linguists is what leads to the extinction of some words from our vocabulary while others thrive. In the case of *fuck*, linguistics offers an explanation.

Phonological patterns are linked with word longevity. In particular, the phonological pattern of consonant + vowel + hard consonant + consonant (often represented as the CV(C)C model) is easier to recall than other phonological patterns. This may explain why the word *fuck*, with its CV(C)C pattern, survived while sixteenth-century contemporaries like *swive* and *jape*, which have different patterns, did not.[116] In essence, our very conception of "four-letter words" may have a scientific foundation. But linguistics provides an even greater contribution to the understanding of the law's treatment of the word *fuck*—the recognition of its various uses.

FUCK[1] AND *FUCK*[2]

Fuck is a highly varied word. Although its first English form was likely as a verb meaning to engage in heterosexual intercourse, *fuck* now has various verb uses, not to mention utility as a noun, adjective, adverb, and interjection. Testimony to the varied nature of the word *fuck* is Jesse Sheidlower's dictionary, *The F-Word*, the definitive source on its use. Now in its second edition, the reference book is devoted exclusively to uses of the word *fuck* and now spans 272 pages with hundreds of entries from *absofuckinglutely* to *zipless fuck*.[117]

Although there may be hundreds of permutations, linguists point out that these variations really stem from two distinct words. For convenience, they can be labeled as *Fuck*[1] and

Fuck². *Fuck¹* means literally "to copulate." It also encompasses figurative uses such as "to cheat," "to exploit," and "to deceive." Thus, *Fuck¹* is referential. Ironically, we tend to use *Fuck¹* more to reference nonsexual things than to reference having sex.

But most of the time, our use of *fuck* isn't referential at all; it's *Fuck²*. *Fuck²* doesn't have any intrinsic meaning at all. Rather, it's merely a word that has offensive force. It can be substituted for other swear words or used in maledictions. In essence, *Fuck²* is the emotional meaning of the word. It can, however, reflect all kinds of emotions: dismay (aw, fuck it), aggression (don't fuck with me), intensification (it's fucking freezing), confusion (where the fuck are we?), disinterest (I don't give a fuck), dissatisfaction (I don't like what the fuck is going on here), and suspicion (who the fuck was that?), to list a few.[118]

The critical relationship between *Fuck¹* and *Fuck²* is the migration of usage. *Fuck* starts out primarily serving a referential function. It's as a sexual reference that taboo attached. Over time, the referential meaning of *Fuck¹* gave way to the emotional meanings of *Fuck²*. The taboo that first attached to sexual *Fuck¹* migrates to emotional *Fuck²* despite its nonsexual meaning. The sexual reference is gone, but the taboo remains. This linguistic distinction is one of the keys to understanding why the legal treatment of *fuck* is so inconsistent. The law fails to appreciate the difference between sexual, referential usage of *fuck* and nonsexual, emotional variations.

Armed with this knowledge, some researchers blend the understanding of words from linguistics with the understanding of the human mind from psychology. These psycholinguists make the greatest contribution to our comprehension of the legal treatment of *fuck*. For the psycholinguists, it starts with taboo.

AN OBSCENITY SYMBOL

An understanding of *fuck* as taboo language begins with Columbia University English Professor Allen Walker Read's groundbreaking work in 1934—"An Obscenity Symbol."[119] Read combined both linguistic and psychoanalytic principles to understand the nature of obscenity in general and the taboo status of *fuck* in particular. He viewed obscenity as a symbolic construct: "obscenity lies not in words or things, but in attitudes that people have towards these words and things." The deep psychological motivation for taboo, according to Read, "probably has its roots in the fear of the mysterious power of the sex impulse." Because primitive man found that the force of passion could so disorder life, he hedged it with prohibitions.

According to Read, the taboo persists because there is an emotional reaction, or "fearful thrill," that generates from speaking the forbidden word. If you use the word to insult someone or to feel the thrill of doing something that is forbidden, you are actually observing the taboo; this is often labeled as "inverted taboo." Thus, the taboo word is perpetuated through both its use and nonuse.

THE PRINCIPAL OBSCENE WORD

It took twenty years before another psycholinguist, Dr. Leo Stone, returned to the study of *fuck*. With his inquiry of *fuck* in "On the Principal Obscene Word of the English Language," all the tools of psychoanalysis were brought to bear on this subject. To Stone, the application of psychoanalysis to *fuck* was natural: "Since language is the chief instrument of psychoanalysis, and sex a major field of its scientific and therapeutic interest, the investigation of an obscene word would seem a natural psycho-analytic undertaking…" His 1954 article was in response to one patient's persistent use of the word *fuck* during analysis sessions. Stone describes the clinical experience as follows:

> Mary S., married, usually in sudden pauses of her free
> association, would state that there came to her mind,
> without affect or impulse, the phrase "I want to fuck
> the analyst." This was usually entirely out of context,
> at first gave rise to mild conventional embarrassment,
> and later came to be reported with slight bored
> irritation as a sort of recrudescent mild nuisance.

Determined to better understand both his patient's use of the expletive and its taboo status, Stone provides both an encyclopedic narrative of the history and etymology of *fuck* and his own theory explaining its use. Stone concluded that based on "inferences from clinical observation, the opinion is established that the important and taboo English word 'fuck' bears at least an unconscious rhyme relation… to the word 'suck' within the framework of considerations that determine the general phenomenon of obscenity, including the anal emissive pleasure in speech." Thus, Stone developed the preliminary idea that the rhyme with the word *suck* might have been an important unconscious determinant in the linguistic fixation and taboo of our word.[120]

PSYCHOLINGUISTIC INSIGHTS

Whether you're willing to fully embrace Read's obscenity symbolism or Stone's fuck/suck hypothesis or not, these early psycholinguists provide us with two keen insights. First, *fuck* persists not in spite of taboo but because of it. As Read aptly put it: "A word is obscene not because the thing named is obscene, but because the speaker or hearer regards it, owing to the interference of a taboo, with a sneaking, shame-faced, psychopathic attitude."[121]

Having set aside the word *fuck* as an obscenity symbol, we work hard to maintain the sacredness of the symbol. This is done primarily by implanting the taboo in our children. Children are taught a language of discourse—"this is a cat" and "this is a tree." However, they're not offered the words to describe sex. A split world of words remains: "a world of things with legitimate official names" and a world of silence—taboo.[122] Your own experience probably bears witness to this. If you grew up in the United States, my guess is that as soon as you learned the word *fuck*, you also learned you weren't supposed to use it.

The second contribution of the psycholinguists is that *fuck* is taboo because of our buried, subconscious feelings about sex. As Richard Dooling expresses in *Blue Streak*:

> Perhaps, as Read suggests, we carefully and subconsciously gather all the indelicate and unseemly associations we have with the brute act of reproduction, incest, sex outside of marriage, sex without love, selfish sex, child sexual abuse, fatal venereal diseases—and assign them all to a single unspeakable word. When the word is uttered, it stirs up all these unconscious, unspeakable aspects of sexual congress, which we don't like to think about because they threaten the social order in a terrifying way.[123]

Read and Stone may have been the pioneers in their studies of this word, but the psychoanalytic link to sex they espoused is now widely accepted. It finds expression in those researchers who explain *fuck*'s taboo status as a reflection of the Oedipus complex. According to Dr. Ariel Arango in his book *Dirty Words: Psychoanalytic Insights*, "the 'dirty' word, to *fuck*, always means, at root, to *fuck* one's mother; to go back to her womb. Such is the universal Oedipus longing."[124] Because this incestuous desire must be suppressed, a ban on the everyday use of the word that conjures up the idea is essential. By focusing on the link between language and the subconscious mind, the psycholinguists provide a vital link in our understanding of why *fuck* is treated so differently from the rest of our vocabulary. Armed with this knowledge, other scientists are now exploring the physiological and neurological aspects of taboo.

THE SCIENCE OF TABOO

Recent research into how our brains function provides more scientific support for the persistence of taboo words. The human brain has a limbic system, which regulates emotion, and the neocortex, which provides knowledge and reason. These two systems are connected and work together. However, it's in the neocortex, predominantly in the left hemisphere, where the denotations of words are concentrated. Connotations of words, on the other hand, are spread across the connections of the neocortex and limbic system, predominantly in the right hemisphere. Within the limbic system, located at the front of the temporal lobe, lies the amygdala—the part of the brain that invests memories with emotion. When a person sees a taboo word, the amygdala shows greater metabolic activity. Thus our exposure to taboo words elicits an emotional reaction—a reflexive, involuntary one.[125]

A classic illustration of this process is known as the Stroop Effect. In 1935 John Ridley Stroop published "Studies of Interference in Serial Verbal Reactions" in the *Journal of Experimental Psychology*.[126] He found that when a word such as "yellow" is printed in a different color than the one expressed by the word's meaning (the word "yellow" is printed in green ink, for example), there's a delay in the processing of the word's color, which leads to both more mistakes and slower reaction times. This interference is due to the automatic or reflexive process of reading. The brain automatically determines the meaning of the word, but then it has to override this first impression by identifying the color of the word.[127]

Psychologist Don MacKay and others adapted the Stroop Effect to test interference caused by taboo words. Instead of using the words for colors (like *red*, *green*, and *blue*), Mackay uses taboo words (*shit*, *cunt*, and *fuck*), which are printed in different ink colors. He found that taboo words also caused interference leading to both error and delay in reaction time.[128] Again, this was an automatic, emotional response inherent to speech and reading perception. When confronted with a taboo word, the brain automatically processes its meaning, including unpleasant, emotional connotations.

Recently, Harvard's Steven Pinker described how we react when confronted by taboo language: "The response is not only emotional but involuntary. It's not just that we don't have earlids to shut out unwanted sounds. Once a word is seen or heard, we are incapable of treating it as a squiggle or noise; we reflexively look it up in memory and respond to its meaning, including its connotation."[129]

Research into the neurological disorder known as coprolalia, the involuntary utterance of dirty words, supports the link between taboo words and the emotional processing center of the brain, the limbic system. People suffering from Tourette's syndrome, a disorder manifesting in repeated vocal tics, often exhibit coprolalia. Sufferers of this disorder curse profusely in what appear to be emotional outbursts. Research into this disorder now indicates the outbursts of dirty words are caused by a breakdown of the brain's ability to inhibit parts of the limbic system. In their book, *Forbidden Words*, linguists Keith Allan and Kate Burridge conclude:

> There may not yet be any laboratory or neuro-imaging studies that have conclusively identified the exact neuro-anatomical sites where taboo expressions are stored, or that have evaluated specifically the neurological processing of obscenities, but the evidence seems overwhelming: taboo language is rooted deeply in human neural anatomy; it is inbuilt, hard-wired into the limbic systems of our brains.[130]

By applying the basic research findings of linguists, psycholinguists, and other scientists who study taboo, we gain insight into both the way we react to *fuck* and why we have that reaction. When confronted with the word *fuck*, we respond automatically. This reflexive response is to *fuck*'s denotations and connotations. Regardless of whether we hear *Fuck*[1] or *Fuck*[2], the mind unpacks all the emotional baggage about sex that is culturally contained in the four-letter word.

Just as Pandora opened her jar and released its evils—greed, vanity, slander, and envy—our mind opens the word *fuck* and releases the horribles associated with sex—rape, incest, unwanted pregnancy, venereal disease, adultery, sodomy, child abuse, illegitimacy, and the like.

SUBCONSCIOUS MIND, CONSCIOUS REACTION

Although our subconscious mind travels this dark path, we still have conscious choices on how we'll react to *fuck*. It's with these choices, first by individuals and later by institutions, that taboo is fortified or conquered. As you'll see in the next chapter, those who experience an extreme emotional reaction to taboo aren't satisfied with cleaning up their own language; they want to wash out your mouth as well.

CHAPTER SIX

Fuck Fetish

When you hear *fuck*, your brain automatically produces an emotional reaction to the word's taboo—all those unhealthy feelings and fears about sex. You can't stop this reflexive processing of the taboo, but you do have choices on how to react. Will you conform to the taboo by self-censoring your own speech? Or work to expand taboo by trying to clean up your neighbor's vocabulary? Or use *fuck* for its shock value? Or choose a euphemism? It's with these choices, first by individuals and later by institutions, that word taboo itself is institutionalized.

SELF-CENSORING

One reaction to taboo is to adhere to it. Those who refrain from saying *fuck* because of the taboo engage in self-censoring. It is important here to understand this distinction: Censoring differs from censorship. Institutional suppression of language is censorship, such as when the Federal Communication Commission prohibits broadcasting the word *fuck*. Censoring occurs when individuals decide not to say certain words. We all engage in some level of language censoring. You can't just say everything that pops into your head. To avoid confronting *fuck*'s fears and feelings, one can simply self-censor and forgo saying *fuck*. This choice, of course, is word taboo.

EUPHEMISM AND THE F-WORD

A second potential response is a corollary of self-censoring—the use of euphemisms. A euphemism is a word or phrase used as an alterative to a taboo word. While the euphemism concept is likely familiar to you, its two siblings, dysphemism and orthophemism, are probably not. If a euphemism is a "sweet talk" substitute, a dysphemism is an offensive substitute. Words we might consider as taboo words come from the pool of dysphemisms. An orthophemism is a straight-talking alternative—not overly polite or sweet-sounding or offensive. For example, *intercourse* is an orthophemism, *fuck* is the dysphemism, and *make love* is a euphemism. This trilogy of "-phemisms" is used to explain levels of politeness in language.[131] Typically, a speaker would use a euphemism to avoid being embarrassed and at the same time avoid embarrassing or offending the audience.

"The f-word" surely is our most common *fuck* euphemism. Presumably, it allows the speaker to both communicate the word intended while at the same time conform to the cultural taboo. This just seems silly. Everyone versed in the English language immediately knows that "the f-word" is *fuck*. In fact, if the meaning weren't universal, the euphemism wouldn't work. So why would anyone choose "the f-word"? One possibility is that it allows the user to identify the word used when it's been used by others without emoting the hostility that *Fuck*[2] often contains. The euphemism serves as a filter, preserving a politeness in our discourse. However, such a quoting use would already make clear that the words were attributable to someone else. No reasonable person would hold the quoter accountable for the speaker's emotions.

Philip Thody offers another explanation in his book *Don't Do It: A Dictionary of the Forbidden*, "By forbidding certain actions in which other people too readily indulge, we show that we are not as others are... By not using certain words, we show that we are a class above some of our fellows, as well as in a class apart."[132] From this perspective, using "the f-word" instead of *fuck* doesn't show that one is better mannered. Rather, use of the euphemism is to differentiate class and reinforce a linguistic superiority over others.

It's not surprising that many people self-censor or resort to euphemism. Even those of us with the tools to understand the taboo effect often capitulate. Teachers, for example, who avoid using shocking words in the classroom when the topic involves such speech certainly perpetuate taboo and shirk their pedagogical responsibilities as well. You might wonder, how can you teach about *Cohen v. California*,[133] the "Fuck the Draft" case, without using the word *fuck*? But there are those who do.

Professor Sandy Levinson recounts with disappointment an anecdote about another one of his former students who was teaching government to undergraduates at the University of Texas at Austin. Apparently, the ex-student taught *Cohen* using the "f-word" euphemism instead of saying *fuck*.[134] It's one thing to make a conscious choice not to use the word *fuck* because you don't want to convey any of its meanings or the emotions that go with the word. This seems more a matter of diction than taboo. It's irrational, however, to want to convey one of *fuck*'s meanings and then choose not to because of word taboo. (If it's any consolation to Professor Levinson, my use of *fuck* in this book alone will surely help restore balance to the use of the word by his former students, if not in all of academia.)

Now, not all academics shy away from their responsibility. Kudos to Yale's Fred Shapiro, who titled his article on the value of electronic research in historical lexicography as "The Politically Correct United States Supreme Court and the Motherfucking Texas Court of Criminal Appeals: Using Legal Databases to Trace the Origins of Words and Quotations."[135] In contrast, shame on Valparaiso's Robert Blomquist and his 1999 capitulation to euphemism titled "The F-Word: A Jurisprudential Taxonomy of American Morals (in a Nutshell)." Ironically, Blomquist uses the f-word euphemism in place of *fuck* when he writes, but uses *fuck* when citing what others have written.[136] Of course, consistency has never been the hallmark of this topic. Whatever motivates you to resort to euphemism, there's no question that choosing the "f-bomb" reinforces the taboo nature of *fuck*.

INVERTED TABOO

A third possible reaction to *fuck*'s taboo is to use the word anyway. Ironically, those who deliberately use *fuck* may also reinforce the strength of the taboo. When you hurl *fuck* at someone to get an emotional rise out of them, or because you feel an emotional thrill, you're really observing the taboo. This is "inverted taboo" because it's your use of the taboo word that supports the underlying taboo.[137]

Think of the Sex Pistols. When this quintessential punk rock band exploded onto the British music scene in the mid-1970s, they consciously used taboo language in their song lyrics, posters, and interviews. On December 1, 1976, the Sex Pistols' appearance on the British daytime program *Today* created a national furor. During a live televised interview, host Bill Grundy egged the band members to swear; they were more than happy to comply.[138] However, their use of *fuck* wasn't to ignore the taboo, but rather to use its power to generate an emotional response from the public, and ultimately, publicity. No wonder word taboo persists: both nonuse and use can perpetuate it.

FUCK FETISH

There's a fourth reaction to the taboo—word fetish. Word fetish is an extreme emotional response to the word *fuck*.[139] Those under the influence of word fetish don't merely refrain from using the word; they're crusaders determined to stomp out its use. By extending their sense of "good words" and "bad words," these self-appointed guardians of speech want to silence the use of *fuck* by others—and not just the sexual meaning of *Fuck*[1]. The fetish is so intense that all uses of the word, including nonsexual *Fuck*[2], become targets. I'm not talking about the real "speech police" (the FCC), but ordinary citizens or private businesses that want to impose their version of what is appropriate speech on others. These are the overzealous adherents of word fetish.

The classic example of someone gripped by word fetish is Thomas Bowdler. At the turn of the nineteenth century, Bowdler created "The Family Shakespeare," a version of The Bard's great works with all the words and expressions that shouldn't be read aloud to women and children edited out. Although his sanitized Shakespeare and other purged texts were met with criticism even in his day, Bowdler's memory lives on. From his name comes the term "bowdlerization"—the process of prudish censorship.[140]

"YOU'RE NOW FREE TO MOVE AROUND THE COUNTRY (BUT DON'T SWEAR)."

Just as individuals react to *fuck*, so do institutions. By following the way a few people affected by word taboo can create a corporate response, we can better understand how word taboo becomes institutionalized. The process also mirrors how vocal interest groups can directly influence the government's institutionalization of taboo.

Consider the plight of Lorrie Heasley. In October 2005, she was flying on Southwest Airlines from Los Angeles to Portland. She wanted to give her Democratic parents a laugh by wearing a T-shirt printed with pictures of President Bush, Vice President Cheney, and Secretary of State Condoleeza Rice labeled "Meet the Fuckers." The shirt was intended as a parody of the popular comedy movie *Meet the Fockers*. Some passengers complained to the flight attendants. The flight attendants then asked Heasley to change her clothes, turn the shirt inside out, or leave the plane at a stop in Reno, Nevada. On the promise of a refund, Heasley got off the plane. Southwest Airlines then reportedly reneged on the refund offer.

Southwest Airlines spokesperson Beth Harbin tried to explain: "We support free speech. But when it comes down to things that are patently offensive or threatening or profanity or just lewd, then we do have to get involved in that." Harbin claimed that Southwest's contract of carriage specifies that passengers can be banned for wearing clothing that is "lewd, obscene, or patently offensive." Harbin punctuated the fear: "The basis for our concerns was the actual word used."[141]

The complaining passengers, flight attendants, and Southwest officials who combined to eject the woman wearing the "Meet the Fuckers" T-shirt create a classic example of word taboo leading to self-censoring and ultimately over-reaching. Why did these strangers care what Heasley had on her shirt in the first place? "Meet the Fuckers" is not a sexual reference. It's word fetish at work that caused the passengers to react to this nonsexual word choice. The flight attendants who supported the complaining passengers instead of Heasley were also captives of word fetish.

In the doublespeak from the spokesperson for Southwest Airlines who tried to justify its actions, we have an excellent example of the transformation of self-censoring into institutionalized taboo. Although the company professes its support for free speech, it acts in a way plainly contrary to the principles of free speech. First, Southwest Airlines unilaterally determines that some words are "bad words" and shouldn't be used. As the spokesperson put it, "the basis of our concerns was the actual word used."

But why that word? Would the airline have the same reaction if Heasley wore a shirt with four-inch letters spelling f-c-u-k? I've seen plenty of travelers wearing this logo, the acronym and trademark of fashion company French Connection United Kingdom. Yet I doubt that Southwest Airlines would be so quick to give them the boot. This underscores just how irrational the word fetish is. And Southwest Airlines doesn't stop there.

The company then institutionalizes its word fetish by including terms in the fine print of the airline ticket purporting to ban "lewd, obscene, or patently offensive" clothing. Even if you overlook the lack of notice and gross overreaching by unequal parties, the terms of this contract of adhesion illustrate a fundamental misunderstanding of the law. As you will see, Heasley's use of *fuck* is neither obscene nor patently offensive under the law. All that remains as a potential justification is Southwest's concept of "lewd" speech—an undefined, yet certainly permissible form of speech.

Two years later, Joe Winiecki boarded a Southwest flight in Columbus, Ohio, bound for Florida. He was wearing a T-shirt for a fictional bait shop named "Master Baiter." After boarding the plane, being seated, and readying for departure, another of Southwest's fight attendants blinded by word fetish told Winiecki to change his shirt, turn it inside out, or get off the plane. After protesting this gross violation of his speech rights, presumably to the same flight attendants who were offended by the words, Winiecki capitulated and changed his shirt. After the incident, Southwest's spokesperson Chris Mainz said the employee made a mistake because the airline doesn't have a dress code.[142]

What exactly was the mistake? It wasn't about having a nonexistent dress code because they do have one—a prohibition against "lewd, obscene, or patently offensive" clothing. So was the mistake one of language where the flight attendant confused a homophone (a word pronounced like another, but with a different spelling and meaning) or heterograph (a word in which different letters represent the same sound) for "masturbate"? Or was the mistake that "masturbate" simply isn't a dirty word? Now this would be an easy test. Just don any one of the readily available T-shirts on the subject ("I'm on my way home to masturbate," "masturbation—my anti-drug," or my favorite "Jesus is watching you masturbate") and see what happens. And if you really want clarity, try wearing a shirt from my collection that says simply "FUCK" or "CUNT" and see how far you can go. My point is simple: Do we really want flight attendants to act as censors on common carriers?

Sometimes, airlines turn their word fetish on their own. In April 2007 a Northwest Airlines flight was cancelled because the pilot was yelling "fuck" during a cell phone call while passengers were boarding.[143] The pilot apparently started the heated phone call in the cockpit and later moved it to the locked lavatory to finish. Witnesses said the pilot was saying "F this and F that." When he was confronted by passengers, he began cursing at them. According to Northwest, the pilot was removed from the flight pending an investigation.

In the end, a private company engaged in a very public regulated industry determines what words you can use. It can even enforce its language control by punishing citizen travelers who breach Southwest's unknown language restrictions. And it can do so in an arbitrary way. Of course, the ultimate hypocrisy is that Southwest got its start in 1971 as "the love airline," complete with sexy flight attendants in hot pants.

MUSICAL TABOO

Popular music is another fertile ground for this type of vigilante censorship. In 1984 a punk band named the Dicks released a 7-inch record (back in the days of vinyl) titled *Peace?* that included a timeless anthem, "No Fuckin' War." However, the company that printed the record jacket was offended, so it blacked out *fuckin'* from the cover, leaving only "No _____ War." Both the hidden lyric sheet and the label of the record include *fuckin'*; only the jacket is censored.[144]

Ironically, fear of censorship by alternative rock bands can lead to greater self-censoring. In order to avoid even more censorship than they would already encounter, several bands have used asterisks for vowels in particularly taboo words (*C*nts*, *Sic F*cks*). Similarly, some taboo words occur with nonstandard orthography (*Scumfucks*), and a few other groups have chosen euphemistic forms (FU's, f-word). In the universe of taboo band names, note the predominance of *fuck* over all other vulgarities.[145]

Recently, some radio stations took self-censoring one more step by banning the pop group Black-Eyed Peas' hit, "Don't Phunk with my Heart."[146] I suppose this is an attempt to eliminate words that might be confused as euphemisms for *fuck*. As far as I know, words that are spelled differently, pronounced differently, and have different meanings are, in fact, different words. No matter, the song was replaced by another version titled "Don't Mess with My Heart."

And don't forget Britney Spears's recent release, "If U Seek Amy." The controversy began in Australia where, according to one parent, "I was astonished and totally taken aback when I heard my five- and seven-year-old kids walking around the house singing 'F-U-C-K'."[147] Turns out the shocked Aussie mom bought the new Britney album *Circus* for her kids as soon as it was released. She felt it would be wholesome entertainment because there was no warning label and *fuck* wasn't in the title of any song. The putative *fuck* in the lyrics is in the chorus, "all of the boys and all of the girls are begging to if you seek Amy," which sounds like "all of the boys and all of the girls are begging to if (F) you(U) see(C)k A(K)my(me)." While the Australians were concerned about labeling, on this side of the Pacific the Parents Television Council sounded the indecency alarm, claiming radio airplay violated the FCC's broadcasting regulations. Despite the PTC's grumblings, radio stations continued to play the song. Some stations, however, capitulated by either playing an edited version that takes out the "K" in the lyrics, leaving "if you see Amy," or inserts the name of a DJ in place of Amy ("if you seek *George*").[148] Still the word zealots at PTC aren't content. In a press release the group states: "Tweaking a word or two would not change the substance of the song and would only serve as a cynical and desperate bid for radio airplay."[149] But wasn't it a single word—*fuck*—that got their dander up in the first place?

The music industry's concern over *fuck* in song lyrics and Southwest Airlines' fuss over T-shirts are perfect examples of a *fuck* fetish. Instigated by individuals emotionally overreacting to language, corporations then pander to the taboo with their own forms of censorship. This move from word fetish to a type of private institutional censorship—significant in its own right—also sets the stage for direct government control of language and institutionalized word taboo.

CHAPTER SEVEN

Fuck Jurisprudence

The law of *fuck*, or what I call "*fuck* jurisprudence," begins with an appreciation for our individual reactions to taboo. The fact that *fuck* is singled out for special legal treatment at all is due to word taboo grounded in our subconscious sexual fears. The taboo attaches to the word whether the speaker is using sexual *Fuck*[1] or nonsexual *Fuck*[2]. Of course, those who make and enforce our laws are just as likely to be under the influence of word taboo as the rest of us. These themes permeate our constitutional speech doctrines, the regulatory practices of the FCC, the environment of our workplaces, and the administration of our schools. Although each of these is addressed in depth in later chapters, let me start by sketching the interrelationships of the law in these areas.

FUCK & THE FIRST AMENDMENT

The First Amendment may say that Congress shall make no law abridging the freedom of speech, but of course, it doesn't really mean that. The Supreme Court carves whole categories of expression out of protectable speech. Defamation, fraudulent misrepresentation, and incitement to violence are all types of speech that can be punished. Political speech cannot. In this dichotomous world of protected and unprotected speech, where does *fuck* fall?

One commentator laments that a person "with four spare lifetimes and a burning desire to find out whether he may legally scream 'fuck!' in a crowded theater will come away in confusion if he looks for his answer in the opinions of the United States Supreme Court."[150] To be sure, the Court's categorical approach, compounded by *fuck*'s utility, makes the task complicated, but it's doable. Generally, *fuck* is protected "offensive speech" balancing precariously between two chasms of unprotected speech—"fighting words" and "obscenity."

In the regrettable 1942 decision *Chaplinsky v. New Hampshire*,[151] the Supreme Court cut out of the First Amendment's protection an exception for "fighting words." At issue was whether the states could punish a speaker for calling a city marshal names such as "God-damned racketeer" and "damned fascist." Noting that there has always been limited classes of unprotected speech, the Court found the use of "threatening, profane, and obscene revilings" could be punished if it was likely to provoke a violent reaction. With rhetoric from the Court that lewd, profane, and insulting speech could be punished, *fuck* would appear in jeopardy.

Lucky for *fuck*, the Supreme Court hasn't used *Chaplinsky* as a blunderbuss against taboo language. Instead, the fighting words doctrine has been narrowed to require that the speech be a direct personal insult likely to provoke retaliation from the average person.[152] So even though in the original case a Jehovah's Witness couldn't call the city marshal a "damned fascist," years later the courts ruled that a Black Panther could call the police "motherfucking fascist pig cops."[153] Although rulings like this seem to leave little of *Chaplinsky* intact, it's still never been overturned.

Obscenity is another speech doctrine with a relationship to *fuck* and taboo. Recognized as a category of unprotected speech, our courts have struggled to define it. Initially, American courts followed the standard prevalent in England, which focused on the most offensive part of a work and its likely effect on the most vulnerable of viewers. When American courts eventually parted with this test, they generated standards such as "material which deals with sex in a manner appealing to prurient interest," "utterly without redeeming social importance," "tendency to excite lustful thoughts," or "prurient interests."[154] Finally in *Miller v. California*,[155] the Court reaffirmed the unprotected nature of obscene material and articulated a now well-known three-part test. Under *Miller*, obscenity requires that: (1) the average person, applying community standards, would find the work, taken as a whole, appeals to the prurient interest; (2) the work depicts or describes in a patently offensive way sexual conduct specifically defined by the applicable state law; and (3) whether the work, taken as a whole, lacks serious literary, artistic, political, or scientific value.

Under this test, *fuck* is not legally obscene because of the *Fuck*[1] and *Fuck*[2] distinction. *Fuck*'s most common use is as *Fuck*[2]—a word with a completely nonsexual meaning. By defining obscenity as inherently relating to sexual conduct, any use of *Fuck*[2] cannot be obscene. Although *fuck* may be commonly mislabeled as an "obscenity," modern obscenity doctrine reinforces the taboo but poses little legal threat to the use of the word itself.

By far, the most important victory for breaking the word taboo comes in *Cohen v. California*,[156] where the Court comes to terms with our four-letter word. In protest of the Vietnam War and the draft, Paul Cohen wore a jacket bearing the phrase "Fuck the Draft" while in the Los Angeles County Courthouse. He was arrested, convicted, and sentenced to thirty days in jail for violating a California statute prohibiting malicious and willful disruption of the peace by offensive conduct. The Supreme Court reversed the conviction, holding that the State could not "make the simple public display here involved of this single four-letter expletive a criminal offense."

To reach this result, the Court found that Cohen's use of *fuck* didn't fall into other categories of proscribed speech, such as fighting words or obscenity. *Cohen* was about "punishing public utterance of this unseemly expletive." With the elegant prose of Justice Harlan, *fuck* was protected:

> For while the particular four-letter word being litigated here is perhaps more distasteful than most others of its genre, it is nevertheless often true that one man's vulgarity is another man's lyric.

One would think that's the end of it. The Supreme Court says you can say *fuck*. It's not obscenity. Its use without more isn't fighting words. If the Supreme Court says that you have a right to wear "Fuck the Draft" on a jacket in a courthouse, how can Southwest Airlines get away with keeping a passenger from wearing a T-shirt that says "Meet the Fuckers"? Simple. The taboo effect of a word like *fuck* isn't going to be broken by a Supreme Court vote.

Despite the victory in *Cohen*, it didn't take long for the Supreme Court to create another category of lesser-protected speech to contain *fuck*: indecency. Comedian George Carlin's now infamous monologue, "Filthy Words," spawned indecent speech regulation in *FCC v. Pacifica Foundation*.[157] After a New York City radio station played Carlin's comedy routine, which included *fuck* and *motherfucker*, only one parent complained to the FCC. Seizing upon its statutory authority to restrict "any obscene, indecent, or profane language,"[158] the Commission concluded that it could regulate patently offensive terms relating to sexual or excretory activities and organs. This conclusion is a perfect example of institutional taboo.

Unfortunately, the Supreme Court agreed, holding that it was permissible for the FCC to impose sanctions on a broadcaster because the offensive language was indecent.[159] The Court found in the context of broadcasting that the twin concerns of privacy and parenting trump the First Amendment, so the Commission's special treatment for indecent broadcasting was reasonable. The Court's justification for regulation of indecent speech is transparent—word taboo.

With the approval of regulation of indecent speech, the Supreme Court elevates another player in the censorship game, the Federal Communications Commission. The FCC, however, treats *fuck* inconsistently. In a series of recent rulings, the FCC has erased protection for broadcasters by reversing long-standing agency policies for fleeting utterances, redefining all uses of the word *fuck* as per se sexual, declaring *fuck* as patently offensive, and creating a new basis for punishment—profanity.[160] Word taboo drives the commissioners.

WORKPLACE SPEECH

The important distinctions in the law of *fuck* can be easily upended by those blinded by taboo or regulators captured by special interests with word fetish. The uncertainty between law and its application isn't contained solely in our speech doctrines. Private employers and public schools also chill workplace and school speech as judicial uncertainty promotes aggressive speech restrictions.

Sociolinguistic research into language and gender provides insight into taboo language in the workplace. Quite simply, men swear more than women. This means, of course, men say *fuck* more—especially on the job. Hostile work environment claims under federal law often include allegations of use of taboo words. Because men use the word *fuck* more often than women, hostile environment allegations involving *fuck* and its variants follow a standard model: A male harasser directs *fuck* comments at a female employee. Although the federal courts apply different tests to verbal sexual harassment claims, *fuck* fares well.

Unlike the FCC, the federal courts generally recognize the difference between sexual and nonsexual uses of the word. Consequently, the absence of a sexual meaning in all *Fuck²* and many *Fuck¹* situations shields much use of the word from Title VII claims. *Fuck* and *motherfucker* are considered gender-neutral and nonsexual.[161] Offensive comments that have no sexual connotation, such as "you're a fucking idiot" or "can't you fucking read," also fail to make a case for sexual harassment.[162] If the federal courts can routinely distinguish between the varying uses of *fuck* in Title VII cases, there's no reason that this recognition shouldn't be universally recognized in the law.

Even though *fuck* is not typically actionable under Title VII, it's still subject to restriction by employers' voluntary anti-harassment plans. Despite the dearth of empirical support that taboo words cause any harm to the listener, employers can—and do—adopt policies designed to curb workplace harassment, but that are overly broad and unnecessarily and improperly restrict free speech rights in the workplace.[163] This is another example of word taboo at work. Employers who adopt overly restrictive workplace speech policies engage in self-censoring and ultimately institutionalized taboo.

SCHOOL SPEECH

As we move from the workplace to our schools, the same sort of censorship and chill based on word taboo exists. It may be axiomatic that students "do not shed their constitutional rights to freedom of speech or expression at the schoolhouse gate,"[164] but First Amendment rights of students certainly aren't coextensive with adults either. Student speech on core political issues is tolerated unless there's substantial interference with school activities.[165] Sexual innuendo, lewd, or vulgar speech, however, can be constitutionally punished as contrary to the school's basic educational mission.[166] *Fuck* falls into this expansive and ambiguous lewd-and-vulgar school speech category.

Where teacher speech is involved, a majority of federal appellate circuits exclude in-class speech of teachers from any First Amendment protection whatsoever.[167] In these jurisdictions, teachers are stripped of First Amendment academic freedom arguments to protect curricular decisions to use *fuck* in class. Other courts require a reasonable relationship to a legitimate pedagogical concern before permitting schools to silence teacher curricular choice.[168] The vastly different treatment afforded teachers' in-class use of *fuck* undoubtedly reflects the influence of taboo on the parents, administrators, and judges who comprise the front line of First Amendment confrontation.

Surely in the world of higher education, the tolerance afforded by academic freedom must provide a safe haven for the use of *fuck*. I am, of course, banking on some modicum of personal protection—especially in the context of legal education. Unfortunately, college professors operate in the same void as high school teachers. Consequently, the higher education landscape is the same familiar terrain.

THE CHILLING EFFECT OF CONFUSION

Are you confused? I wouldn't be surprised. What exactly does the law permit? Let's take a look:

- **Fuck the Draft.** Yes, says the Supreme Court in *Cohen*.
- **Fuck Hitler.** Yes, says the FCC in *Saving Private Ryan*.[169]
- **Fuck the ump.** No, says the Supreme Court in *Pacifica*.
- **Fucking orders.** Yes, says the FCC in *Saving Private Ryan*.[170]
- **Fucking brilliant.** No, says the FCC in *Golden Globe II*.[171]
- **Fucking genius.** Yes, says the FCC in *Saving Private Ryan*.[172]

- **Fucking idiot.** Yes, says the D.C. Circuit in a Title VII case.[173]
- **Stupid motherfuckers.** No, says the Fifth Circuit when a college teacher used it outside of class to describe the Board of Regents.[174]
- **Goddamn motherfucker police.** Yes, says the Supreme Court in *Lewis v. New Orleans*.[175]
- **Fuck the FCC.** (I hope so.)

The easier question is what *should* it protect—and the answer is all of them. However, the powerful effect of word taboo is at work. Even though there's no perfect way to gauge where the public is on the scale of indecent language, a recent poll showing almost two-thirds of those surveyed use the word *fuck* illustrates broad public acceptance.[176]

Nonetheless, courts, commissioners, employers, and schools—each individually affected by word taboo—police our language supposedly in our interests. Even when they are unsuccessful, use of arbitrary procedures often produces what lawyers call a "chilling effect." Chilling describes a situation where speech is suppressed by a fear that you might be subjected to punishment. A chilling effect is a form of self-censorship that hampers free speech even when there is no law that explicitly prohibits legitimate speech. It is the deterrent effect itself that unduly burdens our speech rights. The following chapters explore the nuances of the government's various legal maneuvers to silence *fuck*. Keep in mind that even if the ultimate resolution of government policy is some protection for *fuck*, the process, the risks, and the fear that are produced can still generate the negative chilling effect. The next chapter focusing on fighting words doctrine is a perfect illustration.

CHAPTER EIGHT

Them's Fighting Words!

One of the things that distinguishes a free society from a police state is the ability to tell the police to "fuck off" without fear of going to jail. But folks, don't test this one at home—unless you want your home to be a cell.

If you're arrested for saying *fuck* to the cops, it will likely be under a vague state law that invokes the doctrine of "fighting words." Fighting words, sayeth the Court, are "those which by their utterance inflict injury or tend to incite an immediate breach of the peace."[177] Meaning, these words aren't really speech so the First Amendment doesn't cover them.

After announcing this law over sixty years ago, the Supremes have been back-peddling ever since. I can see why: Should calling a cop a "damned fascist" or even a "goddamned racketeer" land you in jail? Confused lower courts can hear the same words in virtually the same context, yet produce different outcomes. Some results, however, are predictable. Enforcement is selective. Speech is chilled.

CHAPLINSKY AND THE RISE OF "FIGHTING WORDS"

It all began in Rochester, New Hampshire, on a Saturday shortly before the start of World War II.[178] Walter Chaplinsky, a Jehovah's Witness preacher, was distributing literature and denouncing mainstream religion. The crowd grew hostile; the police intervened. Although Chaplinsky's version of events varies considerably from the police accounts of what happened, it's of no matter today. The record before the court was that Chaplinsky called the arresting officer to his face "a damned fascist" and "a God-damned racketeer." Whatever he actually said, Chaplinsky was convicted of violating a state law that made it a crime to "address any offensive, derisive, or annoying word to any person who is lawfully in any street or other public place, nor call him by any offensive or derisive name." The New Hampshire Supreme Court affirmed the conviction.[179]

A unanimous Supreme Court affirmed.[180] Justice Frank Murphy wrote for the Court a rather short opinion that allowed states to punish the utterance of mere words. It was the Court's view that "such utterances are no essential part of any exposition of ideas, and are of such slight social value as a step to truth that any benefit that may be derived from them is clearly outweighed by the social interest in order and morality." These so-called fighting words joined the universe of unprotected speech along with "the lewd and obscene, the profane, [and] the libelous." Thus, insulting or "fighting" words—"those which by their very utterance inflict injury or tend to incite an immediate breach of the peace"—could be punished if their use was likely to provoke a violent reaction.

It's somewhat amazing given the development of free speech doctrine that the Court could be so dismissive of speech draped with a religious context, protesting in the town square—a traditional public forum—and against the government. Yet Chaplinsky's speech lost protection because it was likely to cause a breach of the peace, even though none happened. Given many opportunities, the Court still hasn't scraped away from this old barnacle of the First Amendment. But they have tidied up around it.

Not long after *Chaplinsky*, the Court insisted that even fighting words were protected against censorship "unless shown likely to produce a clear and present danger of a serious substantive evil that rises far above public inconvenience, annoyance, or unrest."[181] Or put another way, the state must observe the distinctions been "mere advocacy and incitement to imminent lawless action."

By the late 1960s and early 1970s, the Court further narrowed fighting words by requiring that the speech be a direct personal insult likely to provoke retaliation from the average person.[182] Consequently, the Court protects speech and reverses convictions premised on the fighting words doctrine even when streams of dirty words spew out in anger.

So even though you can't call the city marshal a "damned fascist," and "god-damned racketeer":

- You can call teachers "motherfuckers" at a school board meeting (1972),[183]
- A Black Panther can call the police "motherfucking fascist pig cops" (1972),[184]
- An antiwar demonstrator can say "We'll take the fucking street later" to a sheriff (1973),[185] and
- A mother can yell "goddamn motherfucker police" as they arrest her son (1974).[186]

As these examples illustrate, the Court grew increasingly impatient at the lack of tolerance shown by the police in handling these situations. This may account for cases like *Gooding v. Wilson*,[187] where the Court reversed the conviction of man who said to police, "White son of a bitch, I'll kill you," "You son of a bitch, I'll choke you to death," and "You son of a bitch, if you ever put your hands on me again, I'll cut you all to pieces." In a concurring opinion in *Lewis v. City of New Orleans*, Justice Lewis Powell suggested that fighting words might require a narrower application in cases involving words addressed to a police officer, because "a properly trained officer may reasonably be expected to 'exercise a higher degree of restraint' than the average citizen, and thus be less likely to respond belligerently to 'fighting words.'"[188]

HEROES IN HOUSTON

Finally, in 1987, the Court made this final leap in *Houston v. Hill*.[189] Gay rights activist Raymond Wayne Hill, former executive director of the Houston Human Rights League, was arrested in the Montrose area of Houston after shouting "abuses" at a Houston cop. Hill challenged the constitutionality of the Houston ordinance used to arrest him, which made it "unlawful for any person to assault, strike or in any manner oppose, molest, abuse or interrupt any policeman in the execution of his duty." The Fifth Circuit tossed the ordinance overbroad. The Supreme Court agreed:

> Today's decision reflects the constitutional requirement that, in the face of verbal challenges to police action, officers and municipalities must respond with restraint. We are mindful that the preservation of liberty depends in part upon the maintenance of social order. But the First Amendment recognizes, wisely we think, that a certain amount of expressive disorder not only is inevitable in a society committed to individual freedom, but must itself be protected if that freedom would survive.[190]

On a personal note: I moved to Houston in 1982 when the events of this case were unfolding. The Houston police had a notorious reputation for harassment of the gay community, as well as other minority communities. I recall the antipolice rallies and chants of "Blue by day, White by night." It takes a special person to be willing to stand up in the face of certain arrest to challenge illegal police action. Such a man was Raymond Hill. As he testified in his case:

> I would rather that I get arrested than those whose careers can be damaged; I would rather that I get arrested than those whose families wouldn't understand; I would rather that I get arrested than those who couldn't spend a long time in jail. I am prepared to respond in any legal, nonaggressive, or nonviolent way, to any illegal police activity, at any time, under any circumstances.[191]

It also takes a special lawyer of conviction to pursue cases like these to their ultimate, just result. My mentor, the late Charles Alan Wright, argued this case before the Supreme Court.

"IF YOU CAN'T FIND JUSTICE IT'LL FIND YOU."[192]

So what's the problem with fighting words? The Court's tweaked the law to require imminent lawlessness, direct provocation, and even tougher skin for the police. They've narrowed the fighting words doctrine so much that there's little of *Chaplinsky* intact. In fact, since *Chaplinsky*, the Court has never upheld a conviction based upon fighting words. So feel free to look a cop in the eye and tell him that the Constitution allows you to tell him to "fuck off," and you'll be right. But be prepared to be arrested, go to jail, litigate for five years, and with luck join the "fighting words hall of fame" above. Those of us without the wherewithal or will for an extensive court battle suffer a different fate.

That is because it's not the Supreme Court you have to worry about; they get it right. The same goes for the bulk of the federal courts. But what about the thousands of state and local courts that form the front line in dealing with these arrests? Because *Chaplinsky*'s never been overturned, it dangles like the sword of Damocles over your head. State appellate courts across the country continue to struggle with these cases. Remember Timothy Boomer, the cursing canoeist? He was convicted of saying "fuck" in front of women and children by a municipal court. In his first appeal, the appellate judge affirmed. It was only after the case made its way to a three-judge panel of the Michigan Court of Appeals did Boomer get justice and the statute declared unconstitutional.[193] These types of convictions don't go away easily; the state even appealed to the Michigan Supreme Court but was denied review.[194]

The same fate awaited Patrick Suiter in Idaho. He was charged with disturbing the peace for telling an officer to "fuck off." Convicted by the magistrate court, he appealed the conviction to the district court, which affirmed. Suiter again appealed to the Idaho Court of Appeals, where a split panel upheld the misdemeanor conviction. The majority ruled that "such a personally provocative epithet... cannot be reasonably interpreted as the communication of information or opinion safeguarded by the Constitution."[195] Suiter doggedly took his case on to the Idaho Supreme Court, which ultimately threw out the conviction: "Though boorish, impolite, and offensive, Suiter's statement is protected speech not subject to the 'fighting words' exception to the First Amendment."[196]

The fate of Suiter and Boomer shows the lengths you might have to go through to ultimately get the right constitutional result. Vindication in free speech battles like these can cost a ton of cash and take a lot of time before the case ultimately reaches a court that rules correctly. Of course, this assumes that the state court ultimately gets it right. There's no guarantee of that. The lesson of *Lewis* is instructive.[197] The Court reversed a conviction under a statute that made it unlawful to curse at the police where a mother called police "goddamn motherfucker police." On remand, the Louisiana courts again convicted Lewis. In *Lewis II*, the Supreme Court reversed again, rejecting the state's argument that police deserve greater respect than the average citizen. One can easily conclude that some state courts can't be trusted to stop censoring and follow the First Amendment.

DON'T FUCK WITH TEXAS

Even when frontline courts follow the First Amendment, remember that each reported case begins with a police officer exercising discretion—often influenced by taboo. Consider what happened in March 2009 in Galveston, Texas.[198] A visitor from New York and his girlfriend were eating at a Mexican food restaurant. According to police reports, the guy berated his girlfriend by saying, "I can't believe you're so fucking stupid" followed by "what the fuck were you thinking." A Galveston police officer was within earshot and took the New Yorker outside to tell him to watch his mouth. When the restaurant manager claimed the word offended him, the officer arrested the New Yorker on disorderly conduct.[199]

This sadly is not an isolated incident. In nearby La Marque, Texas, Kathryn "Kristi" Fridge was shopping for batteries at Wal-Mart in advance of Tropical Storm Edouard. Finding the battery shelf empty, she turned to her mother and exclaimed, "They're all fucking gone!" Having lived through several hurricanes, I can attest that Kristi's response was appropriate. Unfortunately, Alfred Decker, a La Marque assistant fire marshal and certified peace officer, didn't think so. Having overheard the conversation, Decker came from around the corner and told Fridge to watch her language. When Fridge responded that her private conversation with Mom was none of his business, Decker ordered her outside, got his citation book, and gave her a ticket for—you guessed it—disorderly conduct.[200]

Now don't go thinking that the Lone Star State is the only place where the police are busting the foul-mouthed. There's Pennsylvania's cursing-at-commode case.[201] In October 2007, Dawn Herb learned firsthand that the police can arrest you for swearing—not at them, but at a toilet! Herb was in her own home when her toilet started overflowing. She yelled at her daughter to get a mop. When a neighbor started yelling at Herb to "Shut the fuck up," she yelled back. The nosy neighbor was Patrick Gilman, a police officer who lived near Herb. He called authorities and Herb was charged with disorderly conduct.

Herb describes her amazement: "It doesn't make any sense. I was in my house. It's not like I was outside or drunk. A cop can charge you with disorderly conduct for disrespecting them?" Yes. That's what Patrolman Gerald Tallo seemed to think when he wrote the ticket. District Judge Terrence Gallagher thought differently. He dismissed the disorderly conduct charge against Dawn Herb, ruling that she was within her rights when she let loose a string of profanities. Although the language she used "may be considered by some to be offensive, vulgar, and imprudent … [it is] protected speech pursuant to the First Amendment," the judge wrote. This is just another case illustrating the indifference of some police, whether on or off duty, to obeying the First Amendment and exercising some restraint.

If you want more proof, let's go to Montana. In *State v. Robinson*,[202] the Montana Supreme Court upheld a fighting words conviction for calling a policeman a "fucking pig" and telling him to "fuck off, asshole." Robinson claimed First Amendment protection to criticize the police under a Ninth Circuit case, *United States v. Poocha*.[203] The Montana Supreme Court rejected *Poocha*, claiming they weren't bound by lower federal court decisions. Of course, the Ninth

Circuit grounded *Poocha* in the controlling Supreme Court authority—*Gooding, Lewis,* and *Hill.* Still, the Montana Supreme Court upheld the conviction. As *Robinson* shows, some state courts will continue to convict *fuck*-sayers unless the Supreme Court tells them unequivocally to stop.

More evidence comes from Professor Burton Caine, who has amassed voluminous research on how fighting words cases are treated in both the federal and state court systems.[204] Analyzing a sample of cases from April 1991 to September 2001, which included thirty-nine federal and fifty state cases concerning fighting words doctrine, he found that "[o]ut of thirty-nine federal cases, not one person was criminally convicted of a speech-related offense." In striking contrast, "the fifty state cases reviewed yielded thirty-six convictions or affirmations of lower court convictions, while only fourteen were dismissed or reversed." When the details of the state-court convictions are reviewed, Professor Caine concludes that state courts mainly "punish ordinary people—principally racial minorities—for talking back to the police." The message state courts send in these "contempt of cop" cases is clear: don't talk back to the police.

TABOO'S CHILLING EFFECT

I have no doubt that speech is chilled through the arbitrary enforcement of fighting words doctrine. What's the reason local and state courts uphold more convictions? The power of taboo speech helps explain here. Police officers, like the rest of us, react to the subconscious power of taboo. Even though the Supreme Court may announce a legal standard requiring police to be more thick-skinned to *fuck* comments, that doesn't necessarily make it so. The visceral reaction to being told to fuck off may well account for arrests despite knowledge that the First Amendment says otherwise. The close working relationship between the municipal courts and magistrates who typically hear these cases and the police who conduct the arrests may contribute to judicial sympathy for the officers' plights. As the adjudication gets further removed from the people and events that generate the arrest—a challenge in the federal courts or appellate progression in the state courts—taboo can be outweighed by reason. At a minimum, word taboo explains why *fuck* and its siblings continue to raise the dander of cops and judges alike. Fighting words isn't the only First Amendment doctrine that can get judges hot under the collar. As we see in the next chapter, obscenity can be just as steamy.

CHAPTER NINE

Obscenity—They Know It When They See It

Like fighting words, obscenity is another category of speech unprotected by the First Amendment. Yet defining obscenity in clear and specific terms is difficult. Is *fuck* obscene? To many people, an "obscenity" is an offensive or indecent word; *fuck* certainly fills that bill. The law, however, has its own definition of obscene—one that avoids identifying any specific words that are obscene. To do otherwise would be problematic.

Suppose, for example, lawmakers want to criminalize any use of the word *fuck* as obscene and punishable by a fine. They would have to use the word themselves to draft the statute, publish, and distribute it. To achieve clarity and specificity, the lawmakers would have to violate their own statute and be obscene. This is an inherent problem with defining obscenity.

COLONIES TO COMSTOCKERY

Definitional difficulties aside, obscenity statutes have been part of our history since colonial times. In 1711 the Massachusetts Bay Colony made it an offense to write, print, or publish "any Filthy Obscene or Prophane Song, Pamphlet, Libel or Mock-Sermon, in Imitation or in Mimicking of Preaching, or any other part of Divine Worship."[205] This law was really targeting profanity; that is, offensive speech that is secular or indifferent toward religion, as opposed to obscenity. So although obscenity laws like the one in colonial Massachusetts predate the Constitution and Bill of Rights, obscenity convictions don't. The first reported decision sustaining a conviction for obscenity didn't happen until 1815.[206]

During the nineteenth century, American courts generally followed the British standard for obscenity, which focused on the sexual nature of the material and its tendency to corrupt those susceptible to it, such as women and children. This standard was clearly articulated in 1868 in *Regina v. Hicklin,*[207] where Lord Chief Justice Cockburn stated: "I think the test of obscenity is this, whether the tendency of the matter charged as obscene is to deprave and corrupt those whose minds are open to such immoral influences, and into whose hands a publication of this sort may fall." American courts, state and federal, applied the *Hicklin* test—a standard reflecting the taboo nature of sexual conduct and language prevalent at the time, the effects of which continue to the present.

By the end of the nineteenth century, we had our own homegrown antiobscenity zealot, Anthony Comstock, the leader of the New York Society for the Suppression of Vice. This organization started as a committee of the YMCA of New York and quickly became its own independent entity. Interestingly, the New York State Legislature incorporated this private organization, giving it power to search and seize obscene material. The group also received a portion of whatever punitive fines were imposed, giving them a financial motive to stamp out vice.[208] Comstock led this vice squad with aplomb: By 1874, Comstock had been responsible for seizing 130,000 pounds of books, 194,000 pictures and photographs, and 60,300 "articles made of rubber for immoral purposes, and used by both sexes."[209]

In 1873, largely due to Comstock's efforts, Congress enacted new federal obscenity legislation. This act, "An Act for the Suppression of Trade in, and Circulation of, Obscene Literature and Articles of Immoral Use," is more commonly referred to as the Comstock Act. Although the statute failed to define obscenity, it nonetheless prohibited the interstate mailing of "obscene" material. To enforce the new statute, it also created a special agent of the Post Office. Two days after its enactment, the Postmaster General appointed Comstock to fill the position, which he held until his death in 1915.

As the postal censor, Comstock concentrated on seizing a wide range of sexually related material that he considered immoral. He was as successful at this task as he had been in New York.

By 1913, Comstock boasted that he had destroyed 160 tons of obscene material over the prior forty-one years. Of course, he failed to note that this pile included the works of Walt Whitman and Leo Tolstoy, along with many nonfiction publications by the free-love and free-thought writers containing information opposing legal regulation of marriage and providing sexually explicit information about contraception.[210]

MODERN OBSCENITY DOCTRINE EMERGES

During the early to mid-twentieth century, support for the *Hicklin* standard and Comstockery began to wane because most contemporary literature could be declared obscene under these subjective standards. In 1913 Judge Learned Hand expressed disapproval of *Hicklin*:

> I hope it is not improper for me to say that the rule as laid down, however consonant it may be with mid-Victorian morals, does not seem to me to answer to the understanding and morality of the present time... Yet, if the time is not yet when men think innocent all that which is honestly germane to a pure subject, however little it may mince its words, still I scarcely think that they would forbid all which might corrupt the most corruptible, or that society is prepared to accept for its own limitations those which may perhaps be necessary to the weakest of its members. If there be no abstract definition, such as

I have suggested, should not the word "obscene" be
allowed to indicate the present critical point in the
compromise between candor and shame at which the
community may have arrived here and now?[211]

From this small crack in the façade of obscenity, a new test
ultimately emerged that was premised on community standards.

Two decades later, federal District Judge John M. Woolsey
formally rejected *Hicklin* in a case, finding that James
Joyce's *Ulysses* wasn't obscene.[212] Judge Woolsey reasoned
that whether a particular book would tend to stir the "sex
impulse or to lead to sexually impure and lustful thoughts"
must be judged based on its effects on a person with average
sex instincts, the law's "reasonable man." The Second Circuit
affirmed. Judge Augustus N. Hand, writing for the panel,
which included his cousin Judge Learned Hand, commented:

[W]e believe that the proper test of whether a given
book is obscene is its dominant effect. In applying
this test, relevancy of the objectionable parts to
the theme, the established reputation of the work
in the estimation of approved critics, if the book is
modern, and the verdict of the past if it is ancient, are
persuasive pieces of evidence; for works of art are not
likely to sustain a high position with no better warrant
for their existence than their obscene content.[213]

Rather than focus on the most explicit portion of a work and judge it against the effect on those most susceptible to influence, like children, a new standard for obscenity emerged concentrating on a reasonable person and a community standard that views a work as a whole for merit.

But what about protecting our children? In 1949 a Pennsylvania county court judge, Curtis Bok, offered useful guidance in *Commonwealth v. Gordon*:

> It will be asked whether one would care to have one's young daughter read these books. I suppose that by the time she is old enough to wish to read them she will have learned the biologic facts of life and the words that go with them. There is something seriously wrong at home if those facts have not been met and faced and sorted by then; it is not children so much as parents that should receive our concern about this. I should prefer that my own three daughters meet the facts of life and the literature of the world in my library than behind a neighbor's barn, for I can face the adversary there directly. If the young ladies are appalled by what they read, they can close the book at the bottom of page one; if they read further they will learn what is in the world and in its people, and no parents who have been discerning with their children need fear the outcome. Nor can they hold it back, for life is a series of little battles and minor issues, and

the burden of choice is on us all, every day, young and old. Our daughters must live in the world and decide what sort of women they are to be, and we should be willing to prefer their deliberate and informed choice of decency rather than an innocence that continues to spring from ignorance. If that choice be made in the open sunlight, it is more apt than when made in shadow to fall on the side of honorable behavior.[214]

I don't think a more eloquent argument against censorship could be made. The commissioners on the FCC, who continue to use protection of children as the chief justification for the FCC's restrictions on indecent language, should take a lesson from the wisdom of Judge Bok.

THE *MILLER* TEST

In 1957 the Supreme Court finally provided a modern, comprehensive definition of obscenity in *Roth v. United States*.[215] After observing that "sex and obscenity are not synonymous," Justice Brennan, writing for the Court, stated: "Obscene material is material which deals with sex in a manner appealing to prurient interest." In a footnote, he explained that this was "material having a tendency to excite lustful thoughts" and quoted part of Webster's Dictionary definition of prurient: "Itching; longing; uneasy with desire or longing; of persons, having itching, morbid, or lascivious longings; of desire, curiosity, or propensity, lewd." With the prurient interest test, *Roth* also rejects *Hicklin* directly by describing the proper test for obscenity of a work as whether to an average person, applying contemporary community standards, the dominant theme of the material taken as a whole appeals to prurient interest.

Even in the mid-twentieth century, the Supreme Court's definition of obscenity as "material which deals with sex in a manner appealing to prurient interest" still has taboo at its core. One could legitimately write about sex, but characteristics such as "utterly without redeeming social importance" and tendency to "excite lustful thoughts" or "prurient interests" would still support an obscenity conviction.[216] The Supreme Court itself struggled with how to describe obscenity doctrine, but the justices did not shirk their duties. After the Ohio courts declared a French film called *Les Amants (The Lovers)* obscene, the Supreme Court granted review and reversed *Jacobellis v. Ohio.*[217] In all, there were six different written opinions in the case illustrating the lack of consensus on the law. But there was unanimity on the process.

Because they defined obscenity outside of the First Amendment's protection, every obscenity case raised a constitutional question that could ultimately be decided by the Supreme Court. To fulfill this role, the Supreme Court held "Movie Days," where the justices and their law clerks would watch the films at issue in the pornography cases.[218] After all, "duty admits of no substitute for facing up to the tough individual problems of constitutional judgment involved in every obscenity case."[219] Justice Potter Stewart's concurring opinion sums up the definitional difficulty and the Court's need to see the films:

> I shall not today attempt further to define the kinds of material I understand to be embraced within that shorthand description; and perhaps I could never succeed in intelligibly doing so. *But I know it when I see it,* and the motion picture involved in this case is not that.[220]

Apparently, the Court didn't see it very often from 1967 through 1973, when it overturned thirty-two obscenity convictions without opinion.[221]

In 1973 the United States Supreme Court in *Miller v. California* subsequently modified the *Roth* test. The Court articulated the now well-known three-part test that: (1) the average person, applying community standards, would find the work, taken as a whole, appeals to the prurient interest; (2) the work depicts or describes, in a patently offensive way, sexual conduct specifically defined by the applicable state law; and (3) whether the work, taken as a whole, lacks serious literary, artistic, political, or scientific value.[222] This test, however, essentially guarantees that *fuck* is not legally obscene.

Recall the linguistic categorization of *Fuck*[1] and *Fuck*[2]. Only *Fuck*[1] relates to the act of sex. By defining obscenity as inherently relating to sexual conduct, any use of *Fuck*[2] cannot be obscene because it has no intrinsic definition at all. Similarly, the figurative use of *Fuck*[1] as to deceive would be outside of obscenity doctrine's reach as well. Even if the term is used in a plainly sexual sense, the likelihood that the additional burdens of the *Miller* test, such as holistic review, community standards, and lack of value, could be met. Label *fuck* as an "obscenity" if you like, but modern obscenity doctrine poses little threat to the use of the taboo word.

Applying *Miller,* state after state has found that *fuck* can't be obscene under their state obscenity statutes because there is no sexual, prurient interest.[223] In Florida, the state supreme court held that *motherfucker* did not appeal to prurient interest and therefore could not be obscene under its statute providing that any person who shall publicly use or utter any indecent or obscene language shall be guilty of a misdemeanor.[224]

Similarly, the Ohio Supreme Court reversed the convictions of defendants who called police "motherfuckers" for violating a Columbus ordinance that no person shall disturb the good order and quiet of the city by using obscene or profane language in any street or other public place. The court pointed out that, at the very least, obscene language must appeal to a prurient interest in sex and, as a matter of law, the language used was well short of that proscription.[225] The Minnesota Supreme Court also found that because words can only be obscene if they are erotic, "fuck you" could not be said to be obscene.[226]

In Maryland, the state high court held that "fuck you" was not obscene language since it was not intended to excite sexual desire in the hearer (a police officer) and did not "profanely curse or swear" since words uttered did not import imprecation of divine vengeance or imply divine condemnation or irreverence toward God or holy things.[227]

The Oregon Supreme Court held that the phrase "obscene language," as used in a disorderly conduct statute, was not limited to words appealing to prurient interest in sex and, thus, the law was overbroad in that it could deter citizens from exercising their rights of free expression.[228]

The experience of the state supreme courts and *fuck* confirm that the linguistic distinction between *Fuck*[1] and *Fuck*[2] matters. It also illustrates that our courts can see the distinction between sexual and nonsexual uses of *fuck* in the context of obscenity without any apparent difficulty. This should be universal. If all courts and government agencies consistently recognized the difference, much of the confusion in the law of *fuck* would vanish.

As obscenity law has developed in this country, an appeal to prurient sexual interest is essential for finding a work obscene. Since *fuck* is seldom used in a sexual sense, the use of the word fails to meet the modern definition of obscenity. This is the happy ending to the obscenity story: *Fuck* isn't obscene. However, to reach this end our courts institutionalize sexual taboo by defining obscenity in terms of sexual "itching; longing; morbid, or lascivious longings; curiosity, or propensity."

Bolstered by taboo, other legal doctrines emerge to muzzle *fuck*. The next direct attack on *fuck* wasn't grounded on its sexual meaning. As the next chapter exposes, *fuck* was targeted simply as an offensive vulgarity.

CHAPTER TEN

"Fuck the Draft": Offensive and Vulgar Speech

In the 1960s the generation gap between America's youth and their parents was easy to see. Everything from the clothes you wore, to the style of your hair, to the music you listened to signaled where you stood in this cultural divide. Use of offensive and vulgar language was just another way to announce your side. A catalyst of controversy like the Vietnam War was destined to be a target of our most powerful taboo word.

On April 26, 1968, Paul Robert Cohen was walking through the Los Angeles County Courthouse. He had been called as a witness in a court case. Cohen was wearing a jacket emblazoned with the words "Fuck the Draft" and "Stop the War" and several peace symbols. He had no problem entering the courthouse wearing the jacket. While in the courthouse, Cohen didn't threaten to or engage in violence or make any loud or unusual noises. All he did was walk through the corridor of a public building wearing the jacket. Before entering the courtroom, he actually removed his jacket and draped it over his arm.[229]

This courtesy did not lessen the effect of the taboo word on a certain police officer who, after seeing Cohen in the corridor, asked the judge presiding in the courtroom to hold him in contempt. The judge refused. The cop took matters into his own hands. As Cohen left the courtroom, the same policeman who initially complained to the judge arrested him. Cohen was charged with "disturb[ing] the peace and quiet of the neighborhood" by "engaging in tumultuous and offensive conduct."[230]

Cohen was convicted in the Los Angeles Municipal Court and received a sentence of thirty days in jail, with probation denied. Although the conviction was for disturbing the peace, the trial judge ruled that Cohen could be found guilty of the use of "vulgar, profane, or indecent language within the presence of or hearing of women or children in a loud boisterous manner," conduct also prohibited by the California Penal Code.[231]

The California Court of Appeal affirmed the disturbing the peace conviction. In a moment of clarity, the appellate court did find that the trial court's ruling on indecent language within earshot of women and children was incorrect. First, there was no proof that the language was uttered in a "loud and boisterous" manner. Furthermore, Cohen couldn't be found guilty of this crime—*he was never charged with it*. However, these trial court errors were labeled harmless because the disturbing the peace charge was valid. The California Supreme Court denied review.

The United States Supreme Court reversed the decision and rescued *fuck*. The majority held that "the State may not, consistently with the First and Fourteenth Amendments, make the simple public display here involved of this single four-letter expletive a criminal offense."[232] To reach this result, the Court first surveyed the categories of unprotected speech and found that *fuck* didn't fall into any of them. This was not a fighting words case because there was no direct, provocative personal insult. This was not an obscenity case either. "Whatever else may be necessary to give rise to the State's broader power to prohibit obscene expression, such expression must be, in some significant way, erotic." There was nothing erotic with "Cohen's crudely defaced jacket." Nor was this a captive audience case. "Those in the Los Angeles courthouse could effectively avoid further bombardment of their sensibilities simply by averting their eyes."

Cohen was about "punishing public utterance of this unseemly expletive." To the Court, this small matter had high stakes: Our political system rests on the right to free expression. "To many, the immediate consequence of this freedom may often appear to be only verbal tumult, discord, and even offensive utterance... That the air may at times seem filled with verbal cacophony is, in this sense, not a sign of weakness but of strength." Although alert to the divisiveness in the country, the Court would not allow discord to silence debate. The four-letter word might be distasteful, but "one man's vulgarity is another's lyric." *Fuck* was protected.

Although I speak of "the Court" as a monolithic oracle, the men who judged *fuck* in 1971 brought to the bench not only their vision of the First Amendment but also their blind spot of taboo. With four justices dissenting, they weren't all of like mind on this case. Harry Blackmun, joined by Chief Justice Warren Burger and Hugo Black, wrote, "Cohen's absurd and immature antic, in my view, was mainly conduct and little speech."[233] Blackmun's "fuck as conduct" argument is hard to understand. He cites the troubling case of *Giboney v. Empire Storage & Ice Company*,[234] which states that First Amendment protection doesn't extend "to speech or writing used as an integral part of conduct in violation of a valid criminal statute." The *Giboney* principle that speech is punishable when it carries out an illegal course of conduct doesn't help justify the distinction between speech and conduct. Blackmun further dissented due to an alternative construction of the California statute; Justice Byron White concurred in this portion of the dissent.[235]

Thanks to Bob Woodward's and Scott Armstrong's inside account of the Supreme Court, *The Brethren*, we can witness the effect of word taboo on the high court's 5–4 decision.[236] Ironically, John Harlan originally called the *Cohen* case a "peewee," while Black initially found the conviction so outrageous he supported summarily reversing without oral argument. It was Harlan's opposition that led to oral argument and allowed for the most triumphant blow against word taboo imaginable.

On February 22, 1971, Chief Justice Burger, obviously gripped by his own view of *fuck* as taboo, called the case for oral argument, but admonished petitioner's counsel to keep it clean: "[T]he Court is thoroughly familiar with the factual setting of this case and it will not be necessary for you... to dwell on the facts."[237] Paul Cohen's lawyer, Professor Melville Nimmer, responded: "At Mr. Chief Justice's suggestion, I certainly will keep very brief the statement of facts... What this young man did was to walk through a courthouse corridor... wearing a jacket on which were inscribed the words 'Fuck the Draft.'"[238] The Chief was irritated; the rest of the Court refused to say *fuck*, referring instead to "that word."

Nimmer was brilliant. Perhaps the hardest part of this case was to convince nine judges, who were not young, to be comfortable with the youth culture of the sixties. This was a generation determined to shock with its dress, lifestyle, actions, and language. Nimmer was convinced that he had to use *fuck*, and not some euphemism, in his oral argument to make his point that its use could not be banned from all public discussion. In the tête-à-tête between the chief justice and Nimmer, Cohen won. If Nimmer had acquiesced to Burger's word taboo, he would have conceded that there were places where *fuck* shouldn't be said, like the sanctified courthouse.[239] The case could have been lost.

Woodward and Armstrong provide additional accounts of the justices' word taboo and the influence of taboo on their votes.[240] Not surprisingly, Burger relied on euphemism and referred to the case as the "screw the draft" case; he voted to uphold Cohen's conviction.[241] Black—who had always been viewed in absolutist no-law-means-no-law First Amendment terms—said it was unacceptable conduct, not speech. Black's clerks recount that it was word taboo that led to the about-face: "What if Elizabeth [his wife] were in that corridor. Why should she have to see that word?"[242] Harlan, who had triumphed over his initial *fuck* fears, now wanted to reverse the conviction: "I wouldn't mind telling my wife, or your wife, or anyone's wife about the slogan."[243] With that, Harlan became the fifth vote of the new pro-*fuck* majority and was assigned the opinion.

The chief justice, however, never rose above the grip of taboo. When Harlan was to deliver the opinion in open court, Burger begged: "John, you're not going to use 'that word' in delivering the opinion, are you? It would be the end of the Court if you use it, John."[244] Harlan laughed. The chief justice waited. Harlan delivered the opinion—without saying *fuck*.[245] Even in guaranteeing the right to say *fuck*, the word taboo was too strong for Justice Harlan.

Still, it is hard to be too critical of Justice Harlan about his use of *fuck*. His brilliance in *Cohen* was putting the matter into perspective: "This case may seem at first blush too inconsequential to find its way into our books, but the issue it presents is of no small constitutional significance."[246] Harlan recognized the value of *fuck* in our discourse and wouldn't allow it to be subordinated even in a time of seeming domestic unrest. It was because of the cultural tumult that *fuck* had to be protected. But the taboo effect of a word like *fuck* isn't going to be broken by a 5–4 vote.

LESSON LEARNED?

Where is Justice Harlan when we need him? Thirty-eight years after *Cohen*, Senator Robert Ford of the South Carolina state senate recently introduced legislation to criminalize the use of profanity. Ford's bill specifically makes it "unlawful for a person in a public forum or place of public accommodation… to publish orally or in writing… material containing words, language, or actions of a profane, vulgar, lewd, lascivious, or indecent nature."[247] The bill has a similar provision for disseminating profanity to a minor. Of course, Ford doesn't define profane, vulgar, lewd, lascivious, or indecent. The penalty: "A person who violates the provisions of this section is guilty of a felony and, upon conviction, must be fined not more than five thousand dollars or imprisoned not more than five years, or both."[248] A felony!

Paternalistic Ford claims to be targeting teenagers to make them clean up their acts. He wants to stop kids from listening to music with bad language—and he wants them to pull up their pants. That's right, another plum piece of legislation he introduced would make it unlawful to wear pants sagging more than three inches below his hips.[249] Ford is dismissive of the constitutional questions raised by these two bills. According to Ford, "We're talking about teenagers. They have no rights." His bills, however, target us all.

Constitutional law scholar Jonathan Turley finds "his complete lack of understanding or appreciation of the Constitution... is most alarming."[250] As you have just seen in this chapter, *Cohen* protects *fuck* in at least some circumstances, so the proposal is unconstitutionally over-broad. Others argue proposing blatantly unconstitutional legislation like this is a violation of the oath of office that he took to preserve, protect, and defend the Constitution.[251] You would think that Ford, a former civil rights activist, would be more cautious before arming the police with such a statute. After all, Ford was arrested seventy-three times during the civil rights movement.[252]

Senator Ford validates many of the themes of this book. He is obviously affected by taboo and captured by word fetish. He is not content to self-censor; he must silence us all. The legislative proposal is an attempt at institutionalized taboo. But what is more striking is that almost forty years after *Cohen*, there are still people trying to ban us from saying or writing *fuck*. Under Ford's regime, I am a felon. And you would be too if you give, lend, or sell this book to anyone.

This is not a South Carolina problem either. So before

you think that *Cohen* solved the problem, it hasn't. The reality is if you say *fuck* on television, in the workplace, or in the classroom, you had better hope that one of Nimmer's disciples is available to take your case. The next chapter demonstrates just how quickly the Supreme Court itself chips away at *Cohen*.

CHAPTER ELEVEN

Pacifica, a Pig in the Parlor, and Powell

The celebration over *Cohen* didn't last long. The freedom Justice Harlan gave *fuck* was challenged almost immediately be people reacting to word fetish. By the end of the 1970s, the Court announced a new speech doctrine—indecency—to regulate *fuck* and other taboo words. The tolerance of "one man's vulgarity is another's lyric" gave way to the exercise of regulatory power once a "pig has entered the parlor."

It shouldn't really be a surprise that the 5–4 vote in *Cohen* didn't hold. The Court's composition changed dramatically from *Cohen* in 1971 to *FCC v. Pacifica Foundation*[253] in 1978. Justice Harlan (the author of *Cohen* and its deciding vote), Justice Douglas (another *Cohen* majority vote), and Justice Black (of "no-law-means-no-law" fame) were all gone by 1978. They were replaced by Justices Lewis Powell, William Rehnquist, and John Paul Stevens—all part of the

majority upholding FCC action against indecency in *Pacifica*.
As the composition of the Court changed, the safe harbor for
fuck went as well. But the justices didn't revisit their holding
on offensive and vulgar speech. Instead, *fuck* was examined
through the lens of indecency.

SEVEN WORDS YOU COULDN'T SAY

George Carlin's infamous monologue "Filthy Words" is to
indecent speech what Paul Cohen's jacket was to offensive
and vulgar speech—the catalyst that generated a new speech
doctrine. "Filthy Words" was a comedy routine about the
seven "words you couldn't say." *Fuck* and *motherfucker*
made his short list, joined by the other five: *shit, piss, cunt,
cocksucker,* and *tits.*[254]

There were originally only six dirty words when Carlin
debuted the routine in Milwaukee, Wisconsin, at a lakefront
festival in July 1972. After the Milwaukee performance,
Carlin was arrested and charged with disorderly conduct. The
complaint alleged that Carlin used the following words—*fuck,
fucker, motherfucker, cocksucker, asshole,* and *tits*—while
performing before a large gathering including minor children
ranging from infancy to the upper teens. The complaint also
alleged that Carlin used language tending to create or provoke
a disturbance by stating, "I'd like to fuck every one of you
people out there."[255] Undaunted, Carlin apparently culled his
list of duplicates and lightweights and proceeded to make
fuck history.

At 2:00 p.m. on Tuesday, October 30, 1973, a New York City radio station played a recording of Carlin's "Filthy Words" routine. One parent, who was driving with his son, heard the broadcast and wrote a letter complaining to the FCC. That's right, from the complaint of one parent comes the FCC's mandate to regulate. As usual, the complaint was forwarded to the radio station for a response. In its response, Pacifica defended the monologue as a program about contemporary society's attitude toward language. Additionally, the station had advised listeners of the "sensitive language" to be broadcast. The FCC issued an order granting the complaint and holding that the station could have been the subject of administrative sanctions.[256]

Seizing upon its statutory authority to restrict "any obscene, indecent, or profane language," the Commission characterized the Carlin monologue as "patently offensive," though not obscene.[257] As "indecent" speech, the Commission concluded it could regulate its use to protect children from exposure to such patently offensive terms relating to sexual or excretory activities and organs. This conclusion is a perfect example of institutional taboo.

Word taboo was also at work when the Court heard oral argument in *Pacifica*. In an attempt to keep the Supreme Court's courtroom clean, Chief Justice Burger told counsel for the Commission at oral argument that he need not lay out the specific language at issue, just as the chief justice told Nimmer in *Cohen*. This time, however, it worked because it was precisely the position of the FCC that the words were socially unacceptable and needed to be restricted.[258]

And restriction is what happened. The Supreme Court agreed with the FCC, holding that it was permissible for it to impose sanctions on a licensee because the offensive language was indecent—that is, nonconforming with accepted standards of morality.[259] The Court differentiated unprotected obscenity (requiring prurient appeal) from lesser-protected indecent speech. As the Court explained, the Carlin monologue was unquestionably speech within the meaning of the First Amendment; the FCC's objection to it was unquestionably content based. Justice Stevens, writing for the majority, even gets the rhetoric right: "But the fact that society may find speech offensive is not a sufficient reason for suppressing it. Indeed, if it is the speaker's opinion that gives offense, that consequence is a reason for according it constitutional protection."[260] Although words like *fuck* "ordinarily lack literary, political, or scientific value, they are not entirely outside the protection of the First Amendment."

However, in the context of broadcasting, twin concerns of privacy and parenting trump the First Amendment. Patently offensive, indecent material broadcast "over the airwaves confronts the citizen, not only in public, but also in the privacy of the home, where the individual's right to be left alone plainly outweighs the First Amendment rights of an intruder." Additionally, broadcasting is uniquely accessible to children. "Pacifica's broadcast could have enlarged a child's vocabulary in an instant." Consequently, the Commission's special treatment for indecent broadcasting was reasonable under the circumstances. "We simply hold that when the Commission finds that a pig has entered the parlor, the exercise of its regulatory power does not depend on proof that the pig is obscene."[261] The Court's justification for regulation of indecent speech is transparent—word taboo. The Court, through the FCC, imposed its own notions of propriety on the rest of us.

The dissenters recognized the inconsistency with *Cohen* immediately.[262] The privacy interests within your home are not infringed upon when one turns on a public medium, like the radio. Instead, this is an action to take part in public discourse by listening. The voluntary act of admitting the broadcast into your own home, and inadvertently confronting Carlin saying *fuck*, is no different from walking through the courthouse corridor and seeing Cohen wearing *fuck*. Just as you can avert your eyes from the offensive jacket, you can hit the off button on the radio.

What of the potential-presence-of-children rationale? The interests of the "un-offended minority" who want to hear the dirty words are ignored in favor of majoritarian tastes. Justice William Brennan clearly understood the folly of this. He noted that parents, not the government, have the right to decide what their children should hear. "As surprising as it may be to individual Members of this Court, some parents may actually find Mr. Carlin's unabashed attitude towards the seven 'dirty words' healthy, and deem it desirable to expose their children to the manner in which Mr. Carlin defuses the taboo surrounding the words."[263] FCC censorship protects neither privacy nor parental rights while sacrificing First Amendment rights. As Brennan reminds us, even though a pig may be in the parlor, you don't have to burn down the house to roast it.[264]

RISE OF WORD VIGILANTES

Following *Pacifica* and the Supreme Court's abdication of indecency to the FCC, the Commission has tried to keep our parlors "swine-free" for over thirty years. However, the inherent problem of proscribing speech based on its content, the Commission's inconsistent rulings, the resilience of broadcast personalities, and the rise of new forms of media, all contribute to the FCC's inability to eradicate indecency. The speech vigilantes are still at it, though—armed with new weapons to extinguish *fuck*.

With the so-called shock jocks of morning radio trending toward more explicit programming, the FCC released a revised Policy Statement on Indecency in 2001.[265] The Policy Statement retains FCC regulatory basics such as: the safe harbor period from 10:00 p.m. to 6:00 a.m., concern for children, and empowering parental supervision over them. The Policy Statement also articulates a two-part test to define indecent broadcasting. First, the material must relate to sexual or excretory organs or activities. If so, then the FCC determines if the material is patently offensive as measured by community standards for the broadcast medium. The subjectivity involved in applying a standard made up of vague terms that are in turn defined by equally vague terms certainly chills speech. As Professor Clay Calvert points out, "The vaguer the definition, the greater the government censorship."[266]

Moreover, the process is subject to manipulation by a vocal minority that can fashion a community standard for the broadcast medium that doesn't reflect the true measure of tolerance for taboo language. Because the FCC pegs indecency to a contemporary community standard, it often uses the number of citizen complaints against a broadcast as a strong indicator that the contemporary community standard was breached by indecent material.

But if a well-funded pro-censorship group like the Parents Television Council (PTC) churns the numbers of complaints, neither the community standard nor the speech regulation is truly representative. For example, in an FCC action against Fox in 2004 based upon an episode of *Married by America*, the FCC specifically noted 159 complaints against a single episode. This large number, however, actually turned out to be only ninety because duplicates were sent to multiple staff members. All but four of the ninety were identical. Only one complaint mentioned actually seeing the program. The vast remainder of the ninety was generated by a Parents Television Council email campaign.[267] The inflating tactics work. In 2004 FCC Chairman Michael Powell publicly justified increased indecency enforcement due to growing concerns expressed by the large numbers of complaints filed.[268]

The PTC is a perfect example of the way word taboo is perpetuated. The group's own irrational word fetish—which they try to impose on others—fuels unhealthy attitudes toward sex, which then furthers the taboo status of the word. With the group's energy spent targeting *fuck* and similar taboo words, they have become much more sophisticated in inflating their objections. The PTC now has a pull-down, web-based form that allows people to file an instant complaint with the FCC about specific broadcasts, apparently without regard to whether you actually saw the program or not.[269] This squeaky wheel of a special interest group literally dominates FCC complaints. Consider this data. In 2003 the PTC was responsible for filing 99.86 percent of all indecency complaints. In 2004 the figure was up to 99.9 percent.[270] It's easy to see whose community standard the FCC enforces.

"REALLY FUCKING BRILLIANT"

The poster child for subjectivity of the FCC and *fuck* incidents is U2's lead singer Bono. During the 2003 Golden Globe Awards, Bono accepted the award for Best Original Song in a Motion Picture[271] with excitement: "This is really, really fucking brilliant." The statement was delivered live on the East Coast but was bleeped later on the West Coast. Initially, there were few complaints to the FCC. Of the 234 total complaints received, 217 were part of an organized campaign launched by the PTC.[272]

FCC Enforcement Bureau Chief David Solomon issued a decision of no liability on the part of the broadcasters because the Policy Statement, as a threshold matter, requires indecent speech to describe sexual or excretory organs or activities.[273] Solomon concluded that Bono used *fucking* as an adjective. His use did not describe sex or excretory matters, but was a use of *Fuck*[2] having no intrinsic definition at all. Moreover, a fleeting use of *fuck*—even if intended in a sexual way—was considered nonactionable under FCC precedent.

Despite the reasonableness of Solomon's decision, special interest groups like the PTC lobbied the commissioners to reverse the opinion and cleanse the airwaves of this type of taboo language. The PTC quickly had the ear of FCC Chairman Michael Powell.[274] Powell made repeated public statements that *fuck* was coarse, abhorrent, and profane.[275] On March 18, 2004—over a year after the incident—the Commission granted the PTC's application for review and concluded that Bono's use of *fucking* was not only indecent but also profane.[276] In reaching both conclusions, the commissioners reversed former FCC determinations, further mucking up indecency law.

In order to find Bono's statement indecent, the commissioners had to find that the phrase "really fucking brilliant" both described sexual activities and was patently offensive. On both these elements, the commissioners did an about-face from previous FCC rulings.

First, they found that any use of the word *fuck* is per se sexual: "[W]e believe that, given the core meaning of the 'F-Word,' any use of that word or a variation, in any context, inherently has a sexual connotation, and therefore falls within the first prong of our indecency definition."[277] This conclusion is, of course, per se wrong. Given the research by linguists distinguishing between *Fuck*[1] and *Fuck*[2], the conclusion that the sentence "This is really, really fucking brilliant" depicts or describes sexual activities is simply not credible. It does, however, reflect psycholinguists' contention that the taboo status of *fuck* is linked at a subconscious level to buried feelings about sex, regardless of how the word is actually used.

Having cleared the first part of their own definition of indecency, the commissioners turned to the second part of indecency and to a finding that, based on three factors, the use of *fucking* was patently offensive.[278] First, the description was "explicit or graphic" apparently by the commissioners' fiat: "The 'F-Word' is one of the most vulgar, graphic, and explicit descriptions of sexual activity in the English language." How Chairman Powell can say this when Justice Harlan said the opposite in *Cohen* is nothing short of amazing. Such a conclusion is also at odds with the *Fuck*[1] and *Fuck*[2] distinction since most use of *fuck*—including Bono's—is patently nonsexual.

But there was no need for wordsmithing on the second factor, whether the use was repeated. The Commission simply reversed itself: "While prior Commission and staff action have indicated that isolated or fleeting broadcasts of the 'F-Word' such as that here are not indecent or would not be acted upon, consistent with our decision today we conclude that any such interpretation is no longer good law." Having eviscerated its own law of indecency, the FCC finding that the use of *fucking* was "shocking"—the final element of patent offensiveness—is not.

A NEW PROFANITY

The permanent damage inflicted to the already shaky foundation of indecency law remains to be seen. Whatever its reach, the commissioners were so determined to stop people from saying *fuck* on TV that they applied a whole new, independent ground for punishment—profanity.[279] This misapplication is inconsistent with our understanding of both language and law. According to linguistics, profanity is a special category of offensive speech that means to be secular or indifferent to religion, as in "Holy shit," "God damned," or "Jesus Christ!"[280] The commissioners even recognized that their own "limited case law on profane speech has focused on what is profane in the context of blasphemy."[281] Nonetheless, the commissioners found *fuck* profane on the strength of common knowledge that profanity means "vulgar, irreverent, or coarse language" and the Seventh Circuit's "most recent decision defining 'profane,'" a 1972 pre-*Pacifica* case.[282] Luckily, the commissioners threw in the last definition of "profane" from *Black's Law Dictionary* or one might have thought they were stretching.[283] Although there are many definitions for profane, including the commissioners' choice, the decision to make a 180-degree turn from the Commission's own prior treatment of profanity as blasphemy is unwarranted on such a slim collection of authority. From now on, however, broadcasters are on notice that *fuck* is also profanity—at least between 6:00 a.m. and 10:00 p.m.[284]

FCC'S INDECENCY REGIME

There you have it. Word taboo drives the FCC's final conclusion that Bono's single use of the phrase "really fucking brilliant" is indecent because any use of *fuck* is per se sexual and patently offensive; it is patently offensive because it is per se vulgar and shocking. It is also profane because it is vulgar and coarse. Luckily, the broadcasters, while subject to an enforcement action, escaped a penalty because of a lack of notice. But there is nothing fortunate about what is really going on here. To enforce their preference, the commissioners engage in bizarre wordplay. "Indecent," "patently offensive," "vulgar," and "profane" are loosely defined in an interlocking fashion that blurs any real distinction except the obvious one.[285] The commissioners censor *fuck* because it's a word that they don't like to hear. That is, unless it's in a good movie or on cable. In the next chapter, we see just how quickly the commissioners undermine their own standards and in the process add confusion to this already pellucid area of speech regulation.

CHAPTER TWELVE

Profanity, *Private Ryan*, and a Prada Purse

The arbitrariness of the FCC's policy is laid bare by a simple comparison. If the government is going to be in the business of deciding what words we can use, shouldn't the same word be treated the same way? If Bono can't say *fuck* on television (nor Cher nor Nicole Richie), why can Tom Hanks (or Diane Keaton or Anthony Hopkins)? Yet the FCC's current policy permits precisely this inequity—with apparently nothing standing in its way. The exorbitant penalties sought by the FCC and the costs and uncertainties of litigation allow the Commission to extort settlements from the broadcasting stations. The major networks, with the wherewithal to stand against the FCC, seemed to lack the will. Until now. Who knew that shit on a Prada purse could build a network coalition for free speech? But before the major networks join forces, the FCC shows just how arbitrary it can be and gives the green light to *fuck* in *Saving Private Ryan*.

SAVING *SAVING PRIVATE RYAN*

Already shell-shocked by *Golden Globe II*, broadcasters weren't expecting the new minefield the commissioners laid for them with their treatment of *fuck* in *Saving Private Ryan*.[286] On November 11, 2004, the ABC Television Network decided to air the award-winning World War II film as a special Veterans Day presentation. The movie's realistic re-creation of a military mission to rescue a young soldier included violent visuals and many taboo words such as *fuck*. In the wake of the Commission's reversal on *fuck*'s treatment at the Golden Globe Awards, sixty-six ABC affiliates refused to broadcast the film because of the chilling effect of potential FCC penalties.[287] Who could blame them? With the commissioners' conclusion in *Golden Globe II* that any use of *fuck* was inherently descriptive of sexual activities and patently offensive as vulgar and shocking language, airing the film with its repeated use of *fuck* and other taboo words would literally be taunting the FCC to fine them.

As expected, following the broadcast the American Family Association and others filed complaints with the FCC about the repeated use of *fuck* in the film. This should have been a no-brainer given the commissioners' treatment of Bono's *fucking* slip less than a year before. Applying *Golden Globe II*, the FCC found the complained-of use of *fuck* in *Saving*

Private Ryan to be per se sexual and therefore within the scope of indecency regulation.[288] *Fuck* as used in the film was also patently offensive because (1) it was per se explicit and graphic (once again because the commissioners say so) and (2) *fuck* was used repeatedly. However, the opinion "saves" *Private Ryan* from censorship because its use of *fuck* did not pander, titillate, or reflect shock value. Rather, the expletives uttered by these actor/soldiers were in the context of realistic reflections of their reactions to unspeakable conditions and peril—or so said the commissioners. Compelled to distinguish, the commissioners wrote that the context of Bono's utterance of the word *fucking* during a live awards show was shocking, while the same language—only more of it—in *Saving Private Ryan* was not.[289]

This position is indefensible. The "shock" factor of the patent offensiveness inquiry is already the most subjective of the indecency elements and bound to yield differences of opinion. Each of us who hears the word *fuck* come out of a television or radio is either shocked or not shocked. It shouldn't matter whether *fuck* is said by an activist or an actor, rock star or soldier, Grammy or Oscar winner, Bono or Tom Hanks. And it shouldn't matter whether it's said on an awards show or in a war movie—*fuck* should be treated the same. Otherwise, it's the five FCC commissioners, imposing their personal tastes and preferences, proclaiming when *fuck* has value and can be heard, and when it doesn't and is banned. This type of arbitrary process is subject to abuse and should not be applied to protected speech. The arbitrariness only serves to further chill speech by increasing uncertainty as to when taboo language can be used.

If neither the type of speaker nor the type of programming justifies the commissioners' distinction, are there other potentially viable rationales for treating the same words differently? One possibility might be the source of the words. Is the speaker using the word *fuck* directly by personal choice or is it an indirect, quoted use of the word? Although that is a factual distinction between Bono's direct use of *fucking* and Tom Hanks' indirect use of *fuck* read from a script, basing a regulatory policy on this difference is unsound. In the context of the FCC issuing fines against the broadcast of indecent language that must be paid by the station, it's not rational to punish a station for Bono's outburst over which it had no control, yet not punish the station that has total control over whether to broadcast *Saving Private Ryan*.

COMPLAINTS AND CONSENT DECREES

The FCC's renewed interest in *fuck* illustrated by *Golden Globe II* and *Saving Private Ryan* also illuminates the structural problems of speech regulation. A single informal complaint—even one without supporting documentation—triggers the process. After forwarding the complaint to the broadcaster for response, the FCC then decides the indecency case without formal pleadings or hearings, based upon non-record evidence. Because there is no hearing requirement when the FCC imposes a fine, it can simply issue a notice of apparent liability; the broadcaster must either pay it or refuse to obey, triggering the Justice Department to file a civil suit to collect the fine.[290] Given the explosion of complaints that have been lodged in recent years,[291] the litigation option is unattractive to both the FCC and broadcasters.

Increasingly, the FCC relies on consent decrees with broadcasters after issuing a notice of apparent liability. However, if the commissioners don't like the results, as in *Golden Globe I,* they can rehear the matter and reverse— along with long-standing procedural precedents such as the fleeting utterance and live utterance doctrines, and justified reliance on previous staff precedents. The long, expensive, and arbitrary process pressures broadcasters to settle rather than defend speech.[292] When the only potential defenders of *fuck* and free speech self-censor, the intended balancing of speech interests erodes.[293] This is magnified by the rise of special interest groups with word fetish and web platforms to make instant filing of complaints quick and easy, allowing a small minority to impose their speech preferences on the rest of us.

WHAT ABOUT CABLE AND SATELLITE RADIO?

There is also a glaring underinclusiveness with any attempt at speech regulation by the FCC. Its indecency regulations only apply to free, broadcast media. The rise of cable television and satellite radio provide attractive alternatives to broadcast personalities who want to be free of FCC harassment. Consider Howard Stern. After years of butting heads with the FCC over his radio broadcast, Stern decided to leave the indecency-regulated media in favor of Sirius Satellite Radio, where he would be free of the FCC's harassment. In late 2005 a dramatic number of new subscriptions to Sirius Satellite Radio[294]—Stern's new media host—documented that the FCC's preoccupation with *fuck* was out of step with the perceptions of millions of Americans.

Even as satellite radio hit the hard economic reality of the recession of 2008, the freedom from the FCC's indecency regime remained significant. To survive the economic downturn, Sirius and XM Satellite Radio sought FCC approval of a merger between the two industry leaders. Clear Channel, the nation's largest radio station owner, wrote to the FCC asking them to force XM-Sirius to submit to indecency regulation as a condition of FCC approval. Clear Channel feared that a newly merged XM-Sirius would siphon off more "edgy" content and consequently cost broadcast radio more lost revenue.[295] This created the rare situation where a major broadcaster was asking the FCC for an expansion of indecency regulation. Now if anyone had cause to be bitter about satellite radio, it's Clear Channel. The radio giant not only felt the sting of Howard Stern's migration to Sirius but also was left holding the bag for almost half a million dollars in FCC fines for airing Stern's radio broadcasts in 2004. Still, it seems to me that if Clear Channel felt that a lack of indecency regulation gave satellite radio a competitive advantage, their energy would be better spent fighting the policy directly, rather than seeking its extension. While the FCC ultimately approved the merger without an extension of indecency regulation, Clear Channel's protest highlights the inherent underinclusiveness of the FCC's regulation of indecency.

Now don't be confused by the FCC approval of the satellite radio merger into thinking the agency is going soft on indecency. The commissioners continue to identify increased media tolerance of taboo words as justification for increased FCC vigilance.[296] This further demonstrates that the Commission is out of touch: Most people are simply not shocked by *fuck* anymore.[297] The commissioners, however, reject any allegation that they use contemporary community standards that merely reflect their own subjective tastes. Rather, they rely on their "collective experience and knowledge, developed through constant interaction with lawmakers, courts, broadcasters, public interest groups, and ordinary citizens."[298] Given contemporary usage and acceptance of *fuck*, one wonders to whom the commissioners are talking.

Even as the FCC continues to defend its censorship based on *Pacifica's* twin rationales—the special importance of broadcast media (especially television) and child protection—a more realistic picture of the broadcast landscape undermines this rationalization. In 2003, 98.2 percent of households had at least one television.[299] A commanding 86 percent of households with a television subscribed to cable or satellite service. That leaves only 14 percent of households relying on broadcast media alone.[300] This data certainly suggests the dwindling importance of broadcast-only format to the media milieu.

A similar trend erodes the notion that all parents want is a little help from the government in protecting their kids. The V-chip innovation and television rating system, although far from perfect, offer tools for parents to use if they have concern over exposure to harsh language.[301] I suspect the number of parents truly belaboring this issue is rather small given that 68 percent of children aged eight to eighteen have a television in their own bedroom.[302] Surely parents overly concerned about taboo language would educate themselves about the current technological tools available before putting a television in Junior's room—the most difficult place to monitor and control. I also don't place much weight on the FCC's position that regulation is justified because parents either don't use the V-chip technology they have or don't know that they even have it. The FCC shouldn't jump in to protect children from language their own parents don't find significant enough to use preexisting measures to reduce. Finally, remember parents also have the ultimate self-help remedy—simply remove the set.

The new speech vigilantism reflected in the FCC's recent treatment of *fuck* also finds friends in Congress. After the Bono *fuck* incident and initial Bureau opinion, Congressmen Doug Ose (R-Cal.)[303] and Lamar Smith (R-Tex.) introduced a bill that would define as profane, and give authority to the

FCC to punish, any use of the words *shit, piss, fuck, cunt,* and *asshole,* and "phrases" *cocksucker, motherfucker,* and *asshole.*[304] Although this bill never emerged from committee, the FCC apparently decided to seize this power anyway—at least over *fuck* and *motherfucker.* Even though the role of censor may not be palatable for Congress, there was broad support for last year's legislation that bumped up FCC indecency fine capacity.[305] The power to impose increasingly crippling fines on broadcasters for even inadvertent use of *fuck* is yet another FCC tool to extort self-censoring.

However, the powerful effect of word taboo is at work. While there's no perfect way to gauge where the public is on the scale of indecent language, the finding by the Associated Press that almost two-thirds of those surveyed use the word *fuck* illustrates broad public acceptance.[306] Nonetheless, five unelected FCC commissioners—each individually affected by word taboo—police our radios and televisions supposedly in our interests. They are empowered by a procedural system that exaggerates a handful of complaints into a frenzied mandate. The FCC then institutionalizes the taboo through an arbitrary process that either censors *fuck* outright or chills broadcasters into self-censorship. What the regulators don't appreciate is that *fuck* is only strengthened by their actions.

THE NETWORKS STRIKE BACK

Finally, the television networks decided to fight back. In March 2006, under the new leadership of Chairman Kevin J. Martin, the FCC announced a $3.6 million fine against 111 television stations that aired a 2004 episode of CBS's *Without a Trace* allegedly depicting a teen orgy. In the wake of this record fine, the four broadcast networks petitioned for judicial review of the order, directly challenging the FCC's arbitrary and inconsistent indecency regulation. This coordinated counteroffensive was designed to overturn indecency rulings against CBS's *The Early Show*, Fox's *Billboard Music Awards*, and ABC's *NYPD Blue* based on use of the words *fuck* and *shit*. [307] NBC joined the other broadcasters, seeking reversal of *Golden Globe II*. In addition to challenges to the FCC's arbitrariness, the networks also challenged the underlying relevancy of indecency rules where most viewers receive paid programs from cable, satellite, and the Internet—all mediums afforded greater First Amendment protection. In essence, new technology has undermined the basis for indecency doctrine. The network strategy is designed to muzzle the Commission.

The networks scored a temporary victory in July 2006, when the Commission asked the Second Circuit for a voluntary remand of the case. [308] The Commission sought the remand to allow the broadcasters and other interested parties an opportunity to file responses before imposing forfeiture liability—a detail the Commission ignored in the original order. The Second Circuit granted the Commission's motion on September 7, 2006, remanding for sixty days for the entry of a final or appealable order of the FCC. The Commission immediately announced a two-week window for comments.

On November 6, 2006, the Commission released its new order dwelling chiefly on an incident at the 2003 Billboard Music Awards, where Nicole Richie exclaimed: "Have you ever tried to get cow shit out of a Prada purse? It's not so fucking simple."[309] The Commission reaffirmed its commitment to both the troublesome indecency analysis, including the per se sexual nature of *fuck* and reversal of fleeting utterance doctrine, and the new profanity analysis. In this order, however, the Commission expanded its control on language and found *shit*—the s-word—to also be indecent and profane. Further, the Commission rejected both the networks' preventative delay measures as inadequate attempts and any notion that it might ignore the first blow. Finding the broadcast media to be uniquely accessible to children, the Commission also rejected the networks' position that cable and satellite technologies have diluted the importance of broadcast media and that V-chip technology changes the community standard.

Although Richie can't say *shit,* a Survivor finalist can on *The Early Show.* Twila Tanner, one of the four finalists from *Survivor: Vanuatu,* described another player as a "bullshitter." While the Commission speculated that the segment aired by CBS was merely promotional, it deferred to the network's characterization of the comment as part of a bona fide news interview. It concluded that "regardless of whether such language would be actionable in the context of an entertainment program" it was not in this context.[310]

Given this finding, the Commission intends to continue to foster the uncertainty spawned by the Golden Globe and *Saving Private Ryan* decisions. This is obvious even to the commissioners themselves: in a separate statement, Commissioner Jonathan Adelstein chastised his fellow commissioners for failing to develop a "consistent and coherent indecency enforcement policy."[311]

There was, however, at least one broadcast with which the Commission didn't have to struggle. In December 2006, the Second Circuit allowed C-SPAN to broadcast the oral arguments in the appeal of the omnibus order.[312] Given the major networks' involvement, I thought we might even hear *fuck* on the evening news—something that is theoretically permissible under even the current FCC guidelines.

Although the anchors of the evening news may not have said *fuck*, it was used aplenty during the oral argument in *Fox Television Stations, Inc. v. FCC*.[313] On December 20, 2006, a three-judge panel of the Second Circuit composed of Rosemary Pooler, Pierre Leval, and Peter Hall heard the appeal. Carter Phillips, counsel for Fox Television, opened oral argument with the following statement:

> In 2002 the renowned actress and singer Cher responded to her critics in a television show by saying "fuck 'em." In 2003 Nicole Richie, who is an actress, commented on her own television show, which is titled *The Simple Life,* by saying it was hardly all that

simple because does anybody know how hard it is to
get, how "fuckin" hard it is to get cow shit out of a
Prada purse.

Phillips continued to use *fuck, motherfucker,* and *shit*
throughout his argument. Phillips, like Nimmer in *Cohen,* set
the tone for the argument with the use of frank language.
The panel members also used the words, not euphemisms,
when asking questions. In stark contrast, the first words out
of FCC counsel Eric Miller's mouth were: "All that is before
the court here is two adjudications. In both of these cases,
the Fox television network broadcast the f-word on prime
time television." Given that the court and opposing counsel
all used the specific words in question, Miller's use of "the
f-word" sounded silly.

SECOND CIRCUIT FINDS FOR FOX

I imagine the FCC's counsel was feeling a variety of emotions
on June 4, 2007, when a split panel of the Second Circuit
ruled in favor of the broadcasters. Basing its ruling on
administrative law, the majority held that the FCC had failed
to articulate a reasoned basis for the new fleeting expletives
policy, which was a significant departure from the FCC's
thirty-year-old policy of allowing a fleeting use of vulgar
language. Consequently, the court held the FCC's new policy
regarding fleeting expletives was arbitrary and capricious
under the Administrative Procedure Act and remanded the

matter to the Commission to allow the FCC, if it could, to articulate a reasoned basis for its action.

The court also criticized the Commission's new profanity policy as "supported by even less analysis, reasoned or not."[314] The court noted that the Commission set forth no independent reasons that would justify its newly expanded definition of "profane" speech, nor did it attempt any explanation for why this separate ban on profanity was even necessary. This was especially true given that prior to 2004, the Commission took the view that a separate ban on profane speech was unconstitutional.

Even greater victory for the networks comes from the court's dictum on the First Amendment issues raised by the broadcasters. The court of appeals strongly intimated that if the FCC were to simply pass its rule again with a more developed record and more complete articulation of its reasoning, it would likely strike down the rule on First Amendment grounds. The court of appeals noted that the FCC had relied heavily on *Pacifica* for the idea that once the unwitting listener has heard the dirty word, and thus "taken the first blow," the harm is done. After stressing that all the speech at issue was fully protected by the First Amendment, the court questioned "whether the FCC's indecency test can survive First Amendment scrutiny."[315] For instance, the court was "sympathetic to the Networks' contention that the FCC's indecency test is undefined, indiscernible, inconsistent, and consequently, unconstitutionally vague." Although the Commission declared that all variants of *fuck* and *shit* are presumptively indecent and profane, repeated use of those words in *Saving Private Ryan*, for example, was neither indecent nor profane. The court of appeals observed that *Reno v. ACLU*[316] was a similar case in which the Supreme Court struck down an indecency regulation for vagueness. Comparing the FCC's position in *Fox* with the government in *Reno*, the court of appeals observed that they were hard-pressed to imagine a regime that was more vague.

Further, the court of appeals noted that serious constitutional questions were posed by a regulatory standard that's based on determining the merit of the subject matter of the speech. Lastly, the court of appeals raised the issue of whether content-based regulation of broadcasting would continue to be governed by a reduced level of scrutiny, or would it instead graduate to the strict scrutiny standard that normally applies in First Amendment matters.

Judge Pierre Leval dissented because he thought the FCC provided a reasonable explanation for its policy change.[317] In doing so, Leval accepted the FCC rationale that there should be no free pass, given that *fuck* always has a sexual connotation. It is disappointing that this specious argument picked up even one vote given the linguistics explanation of *Fuck*[1] and *Fuck*[2], common knowledge, and common sense.

KEEP IT CLEAN FOR THE SUPREMES

In March 2008, the Supreme Court raised the stakes and granted certiorari to review the Second Circuit's decision.[318]

On November 4, 2008, the Supreme Court heard oral argument. As the first case on indecency before the Supreme Court in thirty years, interest among Court-watchers ran high. I was there.

I heard "f-word," "s-word," "dung," and even a "Gollywaddles" (courtesy of Justice Antonin Scalia), but the two words I was waiting to hear—*fuck* and *shit*—weren't uttered by counsel or the Court during oral argument. What is even more amazing is that this case was about the use of the words *fuck* and *shit*. More specifically, the question before our high court was whether the FCC could punish broadcasters for the isolated or "fleeting" use of these two expletives.

Recall that in the Second Circuit oral argument, Fox Television's advocate, Carter Phillips, freely used the words *fuck* and *shit*. So did the judges. The odd man out was the FCC lawyer; he used the euphemisms "f-word" and "s-word." It was downright Victorian.

When the Supreme Court granted the FCC's cert petition, I was expecting a real showdown between the prudish FCC and the worldly Fox. This time, however, the FCC captured the discourse. The newly appointed Solicitor General Gregory Garre argued for the FCC. He used nothing but euphemisms. (Garre did manage a few laugh lines though, like the specter of "Big Bird dropping the F-Bomb on *Sesame Street*.") Carter Phillips again argued for Fox. But where were the four-letter words? Nothing but "f-word" and "s-word." It was as if Fox conceded that these were bad words—too coarse to utter in the Supreme Court. None of the justices were going to take the lead either. The closest thing we got to a four-letter word was Justice Stevens's use of *dung.*

Without the dirty words, what had the potential to be a landmark First Amendment case ended up being a vanilla Administrative Procedure Act agency review. Following oral argument, I predicted that the Court would likely reverse the Second Circuit on its arbitrary and capricious holding under the APA and remand the matter back the court of appeals to handle the First Amendment issues.[319] That's precisely what happened.

FOX FOUGHT THE LAW AND THE LAW WON

On April 28, 2009, the Court announced its 5-4 decision.[320] Justice Scalia wrote for the majority, which included Chief Justice Roberts and justices Kennedy, Thomas, and Alito. The majority rejected the Second Circuit's decision that under the APA the FCC needed a more substantial reason for its actions that changed prior agency policy. All that is needed is a reasoned explanation. According to Scalia, there were ample reasons.

It was certainly reasonable to determine that it made no sense to distinguish between literal and nonliteral uses of offensive words, requiring repetitive use to render only the latter indecent. As the Commission said with regard to expletive use of the f-Word, "the word's power to insult and offend derives from its sexual meaning." And the Commission's decision to look at the patent offensiveness of even isolated uses of sexual and excretory words fits with the context-based approach we sanctioned in *Pacifica*. Even isolated utterances can be made in "pander[ing,]... vulgar, and shocking" manners, and can constitute harmful " 'first blow[s]' " to children. It is surely rational (if not inescapable) to believe that a safe harbor for single words would "likely lead to more widespread use of the offensive language."[321]

And so it's a "reasoned" position that literal and nonliteral uses of *fuck* are all inherently sexual, offensive, and indecent? The Court recognizes the *Fuck*[1] and *Fuck*[2] distinction, understands that the word's offensive power comes from its sexual meaning, but concludes nonliteral uses are still indecent. The only "reason" I see in such a conclusion is the stark presence of word taboo at work.

What is the reason for *any* regulation of *fuck* and *shit*? It's protecting children from the harmful first blow of bad words. But shouldn't a reasoned explanation have some evidentiary support? Apparently not.

There are some propositions for which scant empirical evidence can be marshaled, and the harmful effect of broadcast profanity on children is one of them. Here it suffices to know that children mimic the behavior they observe—or at least the behavior that is presented to them as normal and appropriate. Programming replete with one-word indecent expletives will tend to produce children who use (at least) one-word indecent expletives.[322]

Finally, on the FCC's conclusion that broadcasters would increase use of expletives if it retrained its previous policy, Scalia concedes a complete absence of evidence. Nonetheless, "the agency's predictive judgment (which merits deference) makes entire sense. To predict that complete immunity for fleeting expletives, ardently desired by broadcasters, will lead to a substantial increase in fleeting expletives seems to us an exercise in logic rather than clairvoyance."[323] Except experience under the previous fleeting expletive exception is to the contrary. There has been no barrage of expletives under the old FCC safe harbor.

While the majority's acceptance of the FCC's explanation of its policy shift bothers me (and the four dissenters), it's to be expected under the deferential standard of review applied in this type of agency matter. There is no such deference to constitutional questions. The Court, however, didn't reach the First Amendment problem. Because the Second Circuit didn't definitively rule on the constitutionality of the FCC orders, the Court refused to "rush to judgment without a lower court opinion." Consequently, the Court remanded the case back to the Second Circuit where the parties are certain to battle once again on the First Amendment issues. And we'll all be back in front of the Court in a term or two with the real question: how is it constitutional for five unelected FCC commissioners to impose a content-based restriction on speech that is unquestionably protected by the First Amendment?[324] Scalia foreshadows as much: "It is conceivable that the

Commission's orders may cause some broadcasters to avoid certain language that is beyond the Commission's reach under the Constitution. Whether that is so, and, if so, whether it is unconstitutional, will be determined soon enough, perhaps in this very case. Meanwhile, any chilled references to excretory and sexual material "surely lie at the periphery of First Amendment concern."[325]

INDECENCY UNCERTAINTY

With the ultimate resolution of these legal challenges still pending, it's difficult to predict where indecency law will end up. Or maybe not. New appointments to the FCC could temper the agency's aggressiveness. And if it's okay for the agency to flip-flop on fleeting expletives, they can certainly flip back. Or maybe there's an unlikely hero for *fuck* in the future. Justice Clarence Thomas voted with the majority in *Fox* but wrote a special concurring opinion.[326] He described the deep intrusion into the First Amendment rights of broadcasters that the Court's precedents like *Pacifica* allowed. He highlighted the inconsistency that allows treating different broadcast mediums differently. Justice Thomas also called attention to the dramatic changes in factual circumstances due to technological advancements: a larger broadcasting spectrum, bundling of broadcast media with cable and satellite, and Internet access. Given all these circumstances, Justice Thomas declared himself open to reconsideration of *Pacifica* in the proper case. Until that time, one thing is sure. *Fuck* will continue to face a hostile

Commission supported by vocal minorities—all influenced by word taboo.

The power of word taboo doesn't just play out on your television and radio. There are other battlegrounds where the stakes are just as high. Confusing speech regulations certainly follow you to work and school. Our next chapter gives you on-the-job training on just how problematic protecting *fuck* in the workplace can be.

CHAPTER THIRTEEN

Genderspeak and the Workplace

The use of *fuck* in the workplace impacts the law in some interesting ways. In general, men swear more than women; in specific, men say *fuck* more—including on the job. Depending upon the variant of *fuck* used, antidiscrimination law can be implicated. This leads to a potential legal conflict: protected speech versus protecting workers. Just as with the uncertainty created by the FCC's *fuck* regulation, ambiguity over Title VII's reach risks our language rights being diluted by word taboo.

GENDERSPEAK

Men and women communicate differently. Analyzing these differences has produced a flurry of contemporary literature focusing on so-called genderspeak and sociolinguistic research into language and gender.[327] Some genderspeak differences are subtle. For example, research shows that women are more tentative in their communication than men, often through the use of intonation, tag questions, qualifiers, and disclaimers.[328] Others, like the use of taboo language, are hard to ignore.

Genderly speaking, men use more taboo language than women.[329] Research by Wayne Wilson conducted among Midwest college students yields this non-stunning conclusion: "Female students recognize fewer obscenities, use fewer obscenities, and use them less frequently than males."[330] Wilson actually conducted two surveys, one in 1975 and another in 1980, where he asked college students to rate their personal use of certain taboo words. Male use of *fuck* was 84 percent in 1975 and 82 percent in 1980 compared to female use of *fuck* at 47 percent in 1975 and 50 percent in 1980. Male use of *motherfucker* was constant at 67 percent in both 1975 and 1980; female use was similarly constant, but at 26 percent in 1975 and 28 percent in 1980. By way of comparison, *cunt* clearly came out the more taboo word in these surveys. Male use of *cunt* dropped from 1975 to 1980 from 53 percent to 45 percent, whereas female use of *cunt* rose slightly from a mere 5 percent to 7 percent. Wilson's data shows that men use *fuck* more than women—significantly more. There was a 32 percent greater use of *fuck* by men and 39 percent greater use of *motherfucker*. Women, however, find *fuck* and *motherfucker* far more offensive than men do.

The explanation for this gender difference is harder to pinpoint. One proffered reason is a connection to the military.

Professor Allen Read linked the disorganization of modern life caused by World War I to the explosion in the use of *fuck* by soldiers. "[T]he unnatural way of life, and the imminence of a hideous death, the soldier could find fitting expression only in terms that according to teaching from his childhood were foul and disgusting." [331] Gender identity and male power have also been linked to men using more taboo language. Although women are expected to exhibit control over their thoughts, men are free to "exhibit hostile and aggressive speech habits." [332] As sociolinguist Robin Lakoff suggests in her landmark work, *Language and Woman's Place*, "the 'stronger' expletives are reserved for men, and the 'weaker' ones for women." [333]

More recent research confirms the link between gender identity and language—with a twist: There is an increasing tendency for professional women in male-dominated professions to adopt "men's language" or cursing to help secure acceptance as a professional woman. [334] Despite this research, there remains a significant gender difference in the use of *fuck*. Whatever the ultimate reason for the gender difference, it impacts the workplace.

FUCK IN TITLE VII

Title VII of the Civil Rights Act of 1964 makes it an unlawful employment practice for an employer "to discriminate against any individual with respect to his compensation, terms, conditions, or privileges of employment, because of such individual's race, color, religion, sex, or national origin."[335] When you think of discrimination in the workplace, harassment often comes to mind. Interestingly, the statute doesn't expressly prohibit sexual (or racial) harassment. However, with its landmark decision in *Meritor Savings Bank v. Vinson*,[336] the Supreme Court recognized that a hostile or abusive work environment could establish a Title VII violation of discrimination based on sex. Title VII is violated when "the workplace is permeated with 'discriminatory intimidation, ridicule, and insult,' that is 'sufficiently severe or pervasive to alter the conditions of the victim's employment and create an abusive working environment.'"[337] Further attempts by the Court to precisely define the parameters of a hostile work environment claim have proved problematic. Nonetheless, from *Meritor* on, a conceptual model of sexual harassment emerges of male workforce domination and female vulnerability to harassment.[338]

This is where *fuck* comes into play. Hostile environment claims under Title VII often include allegations of use of taboo words. Because men use the word *fuck* more often than women, hostile environment allegations involving *fuck* and its variants follow a standard model: A male harasser directs *fuck* comments at a female employee.[339] Title VII, however, is not the "Clean Language Act"[340] "designed to purge the workplace of vulgarity."[341] How then do courts treat claims of verbal sexual harassment involving *fuck*? In general, three different doctrines are used by the federal courts to determine if words amount to actionable conduct:

a gender-specific/gender-neutral test, a sexual/nonsexual test, and a specifically-directed/generally-directed test.

The gender-specificity test focuses on whether an offensive verbal statement is gender specific. That is, the comment must be targeted at one gender. If the comment is capable of being directed at either gender, no harassment claim is stated. For example, if a female plaintiff is called a *whore* or *cunt*, such terms are gender-specific and could fall in the actionable category.[342] In contrast, offensive words that could be targeted at either men or women, such as *asshole*, are gender-neutral and would not support a sexual harassment claim.[343]

The sexual/nonsexual test focuses on the sexual nature of verbal harassment. In this sense, sexual does not equate with gender. Rather, it means sexual activity. If the statements were of a nonsexual nature, such as "dumbass" or "get your head out of your ass," the nonsexual nature would render them nonactionable.[344] Conversely, suggestions that a female employee was in the habit of having oral sex for money, comments about her anatomy, or expressing a desire to have sex with her fall into the sexual nature category and could support a harassment claim.[345]

The third test used by some courts focuses not on the nature of the statement, but to whom it is directed. Offensive comments that are generally directed reflect, at best, a vulgar and mildly offensive environment; statements must be personally directed to create an actionable claim.[346] Even after a finding under the gender-specific or sexual-nature test that statements could rise to the level of verbal sexual harassment, a court might still inquire into whether the statements were specifically directed in order to deny a claim.[347]

FUCK PASSES THE TESTS

When these tests are applied specifically to pure verbal sexual harassment claims—that is, when there is no other contaminating harassing contact—*fuck* fares well. Given what we know from linguistics, the general absence of a sexual meaning in all *Fuck²* and many *Fuck¹* situations should shield much use of the word from Title VII claims. This is the case. Those courts applying the gender-specific test hold that *fuck* and *motherfucker* are general expletives that are gender-neutral.[348] Uses of *Fuck²* such as "fucking idiot," "stupid motherfucker," and "dumb motherfucker" are neutral verbal abuse and nondiscriminatory.[349] Even when *fuck*-based, gender-specific insults are found, such as "fat fucking bitch," if the alleged harasser also refers to men with *fuck*-based, gender-specific insults, such as the "fucking new guy," the complained-of language does not establish a sexual harassment claim.[350] The use of foul language in front of both men and women is not discrimination based on sex. However, comments such as "fucking bitch," "dumb fucking broads," and "fucking cunts" were gender-specific.[351] As Judge Fletcher of the Ninth Circuit wrote in *Steiner v. Showboat Operating Company*, "[i]t is one thing to call a woman 'worthless,' and another to call her a 'worthless broad.'"[352]

Application of the sexual/nonsexual test to *fuck* also tends to be favorable. For example, the use of *fuck* and "dumb motherfucker" are not considered inherently sexual.[353] Recognizing that *fuck* is used frequently, one district court concluded that the fact the plaintiff was offended was indicative of her sensibilities, not sexual harassment.[354] Use of "offensive profanities" that have no sexual connotation, such as "you're a fucking idiot," "can't you fucking read," "fuck the goddamn memo," and "I want to know where your fucking head was at," as a matter of law cannot make a prima facie case for sexual harassment.[355] Even the phrase to "go fuck himself" is not evidence of a sexual criticism.[356] Similarly, in the same-sex context, the harassing comment "fuck me" when uttered by men to men more often than not has no connection whatsoever to the sexual acts referenced.[357]

Irrespective of whether the allegation may be gender-related or sexual in nature, courts routinely require offensive comments to be made "to her face or within earshot."[358] Consequently, "fucking bitch" may be considered a gender-based insult but would not support a plaintiff's claim where the evidence showed that term was used by a supervisor only when talking with others, not to the plaintiff.[359] Similarly, the statement that an employee looked so good he "could fuck her" did not support a hostile work environment claim because it was directed at others, not the plaintiff.[360] Neither *fuck* nor *motherfucker* would support a claim either if the complained-of language was not specifically directed, even if the plaintiff overheard it.[361]

Considering men use the word *fuck* more in the workplace, it is not surprising that hostile work environment claims based on *fuck* involve male *fuck*-sayers with female *fuck*-complainants. Nonetheless, *fuck* statements as a basis for Title VII claims are routinely rejected using the methods described above. By itself, *fuck* falls into the category of "offensive language" or "vulgar" language. Verbal sexual harassment claims, however, can't be used to "purge the workplace of vulgarity."[362] Even when *fuck* is used persistently, it doesn't rise to the level of sexual harassment. As the Supreme Court notes, Title VII is not a "general civility code for the American workplace."[363] In fact, only when *fuck* is used as a modifier for gender-specific statements, such as "fucking cunt," does it appear to be actionable.[364] Of course, such gender-specific harassing statements could form the basis of a Title VII claim with or without the *fucking* adjective.

WORKPLACE SPEECH POLICIES

Even though *fuck* is not typically actionable under Title VII, employers' reactions to Title VII, such as the adoption of voluntary antiharassment plans, provide another example of word taboo at the workplace. Title VII's ambiguities and vagueness leads employers to overreact. Despite the dearth of empirical support that taboo words like *fuck* cause any harm to the listener, employers adopt policies designed to curb workplace harassment that are overly broad and unnecessarily and improperly restrict free speech rights in the workplace.[365] Employers who adopt overly restrictive workplace speech policies engage in self-censorship and impose these restrictions on others just as broadcasters avoiding programming containing *fuck* do.

Much ink has already been spilled by commentators detailing the potential conflict between the First Amendment and Title VII.[366] The pages of the *Federal Reporters*, however, remain amazingly light on the subject. I can add little to this conversation[367] except to say, as to *fuck*, the doctrines of fighting words, obscenity, captive audience, and the like have been explored and rejected. Nothing in Title VII changes this. Only the category of lesser-protected indecent speech (now bastardized by the FCC) remains as a constitutional option.[368] However, none of the original *Pacifica* justifications—parental control, child access, and home privacy—have any vitality in the workplace.[369] A better alternative is to simply leave *fuck* alone.

The treatment of *fuck* in the workplace provides two lessons. First, Title VII law recognizes the varied uses of *fuck* and the key linguistic distinction between *Fuck*[1] and *Fuck*[2]. The tests that the courts have developed to determine actionable verbal sexual harassment, such as the sexual/nonsexual test, treat *fuck* according to its intended use. Calling an employee a *fucking* idiot, an obvious nonsexual use of *Fuck*[2], would not meet the harassment standard. Conversely, the statement by a supervisor to an employee that "I want to fuck you," an equally obvious use of *Fuck*[1], would at a minimum meet the sexual use test. Hence, the federal courts demonstrate facility in recognizing varied uses of *fuck* and take that into account. This stands in stark contrast to the broadcast regulation by the FCC where every use of *fuck* is deemed per se sexual. If the federal courts can discern the different uses of *fuck* in the Title VII context, why does the FCC turn a blind eye to this linguistic distinction?

MIXED RESULTS FOR WORKPLACE *FUCK*

Fuck-based claims under Title VII show at least the capacity for law to accommodate valuable lessons from linguistics. However, the multiple tests used by varying jurisdictions can also generate uncertainty. Uncertainty can, in turn, lead to employer development of overly restrictive antiharassment policies with the predictable consequences. Whether motivated by a desire to avoid liability or to impose a more sanitized version of workplace speech, taboo continues to have power. However, as we see in the next chapter, the control that taboo exerts in the workplace pales in comparison to its grip on our schools.

CHAPTER FOURTEEN

Tinker's Armband, But Not Cohen's Coat

Having spent most of my life in school—either attending or teaching—I know that *fuck* gets plenty of use in educational settings. *Fuck* finds its way into a public school through the mouths of either students or teachers. Given the law's reaction to the presence of children in earshot of taboo language, if there is one area to predict harsh treatment for offensive language, this is it. Recall that in *Pacifica* it was the presence of children that led to the complaint, motivated the FCC to act, and influenced the Court to approve of suppression of indecent language. Similarly, the Michigan statute used to convict Tim Boomer, the cursing canoeist, required the presence of children as well. Whether based on *in loco parentis* or some other modern need to maintain educational process, schools seek to protect children from taboo language. Our courts, in turn, give them wide latitude.

It's axiomatic that public school students don't "shed their constitutional rights to freedom of speech or expression at the schoolhouse gate."[370] At the same time, "the First Amendment rights of students in the public schools 'are not automatically coextensive with the rights of adults in other settings,' and must be 'applied in light of the special characteristics of the school environment.'"[371] As applied to public school students, there is an easy shorthand: the "First Amendment gives a high school student the classroom right to wear Tinker's armband, but not Cohen's jacket."[372] Well, maybe it's a little more complicated, but not much.

THE SCHOOL SPEECH TRILOGY

There are several different taxonomies used by commentators to describe the universe of school speech.[373] Where *fuck* is concerned, I find most useful a categorization dividing school speech into three types: *Tinker*-type, *Fraser*-type, and *Kuhlmeier*-type, based on the trilogy of leading Supreme Court cases in the area.

There is student speech or expression that happens to occur on school premises. This type of speech is like a student wearing a black armband in protest of the Vietnam War as they did in *Tinker v. Des Moines Independent Community School District*.[374] A school must tolerate *Tinker*-type black-armband speech unless it can reasonably forecast that the expression will lead to material and substantial interference with school activities.

A second type of speech found in the school setting is school-sponsored speech. This is speech that a school affirmatively promotes, like the school-supported student newspaper at issue in *Hazelwood School District v. Kuhlmeier*, as opposed to speech that it merely tolerates. Expressive activities delivered through a school-sponsored medium (or what I call *Kuhlmeier*-type school-sponsored-student-newspaper speech) can be regulated so long as the regulation is rationally related to a legitimate pedagogical concern.[375]

The third type of school speech is vulgar, lewd, and offensive speech. Unlike the core political speech in *Tinker*, sexual, lewd, or vulgar speech can be constitutionally punished because the offensive speech is contrary to the school's basic educational mission, said the Court in *Bethel School District No. 403 v. Fraser*.[376] This case involved the suspension of a high school student for giving an election nominating speech that was filled with pervasive, "plainly offensive" sexual innuendo. Despite the opportunity to clarify the boundaries of offensive language, the Court failed to carefully define the speech at issue. It called the speech "offensively lewd and indecent," "vulgar and lewd," and "sexually explicit" all in the same opinion.[377] *Fuck* seemingly falls into this expansive and ambiguous *Fraser*-type lewd-and-vulgar speech category, but where exactly?

What is the difference between the *Fraser*-speech subsets of lewd, indecent, vulgar, offensive, or sexually explicit? For example, "lewd" is often defined as "obscene." However, under a *Miller* definition of obscenity, the word *fuck* is not obscene because the word is neither erotic nor contains the essential element of sexuality to be prurient.[378] Consequently, *fuck* is not likely covered by the lewd subcategory. As to indecency, we must return to *Pacifica* and the FCC to understand its contours. As far as *fuck* is concerned, indecency applies only if one makes the erroneous connection to per se sexual activity and patent offensiveness.[379] The only remaining subcategories to apply to *fuck* are offensive or vulgar speech, yet confusion also abounds as to what these terms mean.[380] In the end, neither classification is helpful in predicting how *fuck* would be treated.

Although I am sure *fuck* is used by many a student, few reported cases explore a student's speech right in this context. Given the outcome with even non-taboo speech, I see little chance that *fuck* would find protection under the current state of the law. However, if I have to predict how the issue of student-originated use of *fuck* could surface today, it would be on a T-shirt. All the recent student action surrounds T-shirt speech and illustrates the difficulty of "offensive" or "vulgar" as useful tools for speech regulation.

MARILYN MANSON, T-SHIRTS, AND THE SIXTH CIRCUIT

To get a feel for just how messy this can be, consider the Sixth Circuit's treatment of whether an Ohio high school could ban Marilyn Manson T-shirts as vulgar or offensive speech under *Fraser*.[381] The T-shirt starting the brouhaha depicted a "three-faced Jesus" and the words "See No Truth.

Hear No Truth. Speak No Truth." On the reverse was the word "BELIEVE" with the L, I, and E highlighted. Senior Nicholas Boroff wore this three-faced Jesus T-shirt one day to Van Wert High School. The school had a dress code that provided that "clothing with offensive illustrations, drug, alcohol, or tobacco slogans... are not acceptable." Chief Principal's Aide David Froelich confronted Boroff and told him that his shirt was offensive and gave him the choice of turning the shirt inside-out, going home and changing, or leaving and being considered truant. Boroff, proving that he was indeed a senior, left school.

The next school day, Nicholas and his mother met with Froelich, the principal, and the superintendent over the incident. Nicholas once again wore a Marilyn Manson T-shirt (the record is silent on what his mother and the three school administrators wore). At the meeting, the Boroffs were informed that students would not be permitted to wear Marilyn Manson T-shirts on school grounds. Undaunted, Boroff returned the next three days donning a different Marilyn Manson T-shirt; each day he was sent home. Boroff sued on First Amendment grounds. Without a trial, the district court granted summary judgment in favor of the school. Boroff appealed.

A split panel of the Sixth Circuit held that under *Fraser*, the school could ban merely offensive speech without having to apply *Tinker*'s substantial and material interference test.[382] What is most troubling is the court's methodology. This is how Judge Harry Welford began his opinion for the majority:

This dispute arises out of a high school student's desire to wear "Marilyn Manson" T-shirts to school, and the school's opposing desire to prohibit those T-shirts. Marilyn Manson is the stage name of "goth" rock performer Brian Warner, and also the name of the band in which he is the lead singer. *See* Encarta World English Dictionary (2000) (defining *goth* as "a style of popular music that combines elements of heavy metal with punk" and also "a style of fashion... characterized by black clothes, heavy silver jewelry, black eye makeup and lipstick, and often pale face makeup"). Band members take the first part of their stage names from a famous model or celebrity, such as Marilyn Monroe, Madonna, or Twiggy, and the second part from a notorious serial killer, such as Charles Manson, John Wayne Gacy, or Richard Ramirez. Marilyn Manson (the individual) is popularly regarded as a worshiper of Satan, which he has denied. He is also widely regarded as a user of illegal drugs, which he has not denied. In fact, one of his songs is titled "I Don't Like the Drugs (But the Drugs Like Me)." [See] Gina Vivinetto, "Marilyn Manson, Not Kinder, Not Gentler," *St. Petersburg Times*, Mar. 26, 1999, at 23 (reporting that Manson no longer stores his drugs and drug paraphernalia in lunch boxes because "everyone... is carrying their paraphernalia that way. Too trendy").[383]

This sets the tone of the opinion—one obsessed with the stage persona of an entertainment group.

But what about the T-shirts? Rather than explaining why the T-shirts themselves were offensive—where all the court had to offer was that Marilyn Manson appeared "ghoulish and creepy"—the court focused on the "destructive and demoralizing values" promoted by the band through its lyrics and interviews. Using a judicial version of the transitive property, the court found that the band promoted ideas contrary to the school's mission and the T-shirts promoted the band. Ergo, the T-shirts were offensive. Because they were offensive, the school could ban them.

If you adopt the majority's reasoning and apply it to *fuck*, you end up with something like this: the band's lyrics include *fuck*. The T-shirts promote the band. So I suppose the T-shirts could be banned as if they said *fuck*. Giving credit where credit is due, it's the high school principal, William Clifton, who propounded this bonehead argument. Unfortunately, the federal district court and two of the Sixth Circuit panelists bought into it.

Only the dissenter, Judge Ronald Gilman, seems to recognize the folly of the majority opinion. Judge Gilman points out the obvious: Even if the band's lyrics are vulgar or offensive, nothing on the T-shirts was.[384] Unfortunately for *fuck*, Gilman defines vulgar and offensive in terms of *Pacifica* speech and concludes that if the T-shirts contained those words, the school could ban them.

This type of application of *Fraser* leaves virtually no speech off limits as long as it can be traced back to an ultimate offensive origin. No speech—except the Confederate flag that is. Within months of the Marilyn Manson T-shirt case, the Sixth Circuit held that a Kentucky high school that suspended two students for wearing T-shirts with the Confederate flag had to meet *Tinker*'s substantial and material interference test before it could prohibit wearing them to school.[385]

Not all the federal circuits would view the T-shirt issue the same. A panel of the Ninth Circuit, for example, declined to follow the Sixth Circuit interpretation of *Fraser,* concluding that "to the degree *Boroff* implies that student speech may be prohibited as 'plainly offensive' whenever it conflicts with a vaguely defined 'educational mission,' we decline to follow it."[386] The case, however, was *Frederick v. Morse*, a.k.a. "Bong Hits for Jesus," and it turned out to be no friend of free speech.

Joseph Frederick was an eighteen-year-old senior at Juneau-Douglas High School in Alaska when he and the rest of the school were released to watch the passing of the Winter Olympics torch. Standing on the sidewalk across from the school, he and some friends unfurled a banner reading "Bong Hits for Jesus" for the benefit of the television cameras. Principal Deborah Morse crossed the street, grabbed and crumpled the banner, and suspended Frederick for ten days. Frederick fought the suspension first administratively and later in the federal courts, arguing his First Amendment rights were violated. While the Ninth Circuit agreed with him, the

Supreme Court subsequently reversed, holding that a school may punish school speech that promotes drug use under *Fraser*.[387] Despite the clear antidrug context that overlays this case, it is still the latest word on school speech from the Roberts Court. Given the Court's treatment of the nonsensical phrase "Bong Hits for Jesus," who knows what they would have done if they got their hands on "three-faced Jesus."[388]

THE PRURIENT "DRUGS SUCK" AND "DON'T BE A DICK"

Assuming for the moment that devil worship and drugs face a tough judicial audience as far as free speech of students is concerned, is there any hope for *fuck* speech? The answer is "no" if the type of inconsistent, if not downright bizarre, application of *Fraser* illustrated in the next two cases controls. Just as the FCC declares nonsexual uses of *fuck* as per se sexual, courts often sexualize other nonsexual language to enforce a prohibition against the speech. For example, a federal district court upheld the suspension of a middle school student for wearing a T-shirt that said "Drugs Suck!" because the message was vulgar and offensive.[389] The court found *suck* had sexual connotations. After admitting that *suck* was also a general expression of disapproval, the court found that meaning derivative and "likely evolved from its sexual meaning only as recently as the 1970s." Consequently, "Drugs Suck!" had a prurient element subjecting it to prohibition.

The same sort of reasoning led another federal district court to uphold prohibition of an anti-drunk driving T-shirt that proclaimed "See Dick drink. See Dick drive. See Dick die. Don't be a Dick."[390] The court found that the word *Dick* came within a vulgarity exception to the First Amendment. This type of sexualization of nonsexual language serves as a good predictor of how *fuck* might be banned by blurring the *Fuck*[1] and *Fuck*[2] distinction. Given this level of confusion among the courts on both linguistics and the legal standard of vulgar and offensive speech, student-initiated use of *fuck* as free speech seems doomed.

FUCK IN COLLEGE

But what of the older siblings—college and university students—who say *fuck* in an academic environment? The Supreme Court hasn't addressed the standard to use in the context of university student free speech rights. In this vacuum, the lower courts have reached out to the Court's guidance on the treatment of First Amendment rights of secondary school students. This involves application of the now familiar categorization of student speech into *Tinker*-type, *Fraser*-type, or *Kuhlmeier*-type speech. However, use of this classification of speech is complicated by the obvious differences between high school students and high schools and college students and colleges. It's problematic to use standards forged in the context of public high schools to analyze speech in our public universities.

The best illustration of the problem is found in *Brown v. Li*.[391] This Ninth Circuit case involved a graduate student's inclusion of a special section in his master's thesis titled "Disacknowledgments." The section began: "I would like to offer special Fuck You's to the following degenerates for of [sic] being an ever-present hindrance during my graduate career." He then listed the dean, graduate school staff, the governor, the Regents of the University, and others. Not surprisingly, his thesis committee rejected the document. Rather than remove the Disacknowledgments section, the grad student appealed through various university channels, being rejected at each level. Ultimately, he sued the thesis committee, dean, and others for violating his First Amendment rights by withholding his degree. The federal district court found for the university officials.[392]

The appeal to the Ninth Circuit produced three separate opinions and no agreement on what standard should be applied to the case. Judge Susan Graber wrote for the majority and used the *Kuhlmeier* model.[393] After noting that it was an open question, Judge Garber concluded that *Kuhlmeier* was the right standard to use when reviewing a university's assessment of a student's academic work. Because the university's decision was reasonably related to a pedagogical objective—teaching the proper format for a scientific paper—there was no violation of the student's First Amendment rights.

Judge Warren Ferguson concurred in the judgment that there was no violation of rights, but for a very different reason—academic dishonesty. He found that the student's attempt to slip the Disacknowledgments section into the thesis after a preliminary approval was deception that the university could punish just as it could plagiarism or cheating.[394]

In dissent, Judge Stephen Reinhardt makes a strong argument that none of the secondary school approaches should apply. According to Judge Reinhardt, "[b]ecause college and graduate students are typically more mature and independent, they should be afforded greater First Amendment rights than their high school counterparts, just as they have been afforded greater legal rights in general."[395]

Judge Reinhardt is, of course, right. There's likely little doubt in your mind that a high schooler and a college student (much less a graduate student) are at very different stages in their lives. Most college students can vote, drive cars, buy cigarettes, marry, join the military, and legally consume alcohol. These are rights not generally available to high school students. In short, high school students are adolescents; college students are not. Consequently, different considerations should govern review of the conduct of college students.

Judge Reinhardt suggested two alternative analytical frameworks. First is the limited or designated public forum in which the government opens a forum for use by the public at large for assembly and speech, for use by certain speakers, or for the discussion of certain subjects.[396] In a limited public forum, the government may impose reasonable time, place, and manner restrictions on speech; not permit viewpoint-based restrictions; and require that all content-based restrictions must be narrowly drawn to effectuate a compelling state interest.[397] The Sixth Circuit used this standard when it concluded that the university's yearbook constituted a limited or designated public forum in which content-based regulations were subject to strict scrutiny review.[398]

If greater deference to educators' content-based decisions is desirable, Reinhardt suggests use of intermediate scrutiny for student speech in college and graduate programs. Intermediate scrutiny would require any speech regulation to have only a substantial relationship to an important pedagogical objective, and hence greater deference than strict scrutiny would allow.[399]

Complicating any application of current speech standards to the use of *fuck* on a college campus is a determination of whose speech is really at issue. Is it college student speech, or university speech, or a private individual's speech in a university setting? As Reinhardt suggests, it may be that different First Amendment standards apply in these different contexts. But when our courts of appeals have difficulty nailing down even the test to use to answer the query, don't expect too much protection for student use of *fuck*, whether it's in a high school hallway or a college classroom.

But what if *fuck* flies from the mouth of the teacher instead of the pupil? Should the law treat the word use any differently? The next chapter focuses on teacher speech, where there is surprisingly greater tolerance for *fuck*.

CHAPTER FIFTEEN

Fuck in Teacher Speech

Justice Abe Fortas's famous *Tinker* line about not shedding constitutional rights at the schoolhouse gate applied to both students and teachers.[400] Surely teachers, cloaked with the tolerance afforded by academic freedom, must have a safe haven for the use of *fuck*. (I, for one, am counting on it.) As Professor Levinson put it, it would be "especially problematic to say that any speech is off limits when addressing the question of which, if any, speech can ever be ruled off limits."[401] Unfortunately, teacher speech exists in a murky First Amendment environment. As the Second Circuit recently lamented: "Neither the Supreme Court nor this Circuit has determined what scope of First Amendment protection is to be given a public college professor's classroom speech."[402] Public school teachers must follow the same uncertain path.

TINKER TRILOGY OR *PICKERING*

Where teacher speech is involved, the *Tinker* trilogy[403] is often supplanted by the case *Pickering v. Board of Education.*[404] Public school teacher Marvin Pickering criticized the board of education for its handling of fiscal matters in a letter to the local newspaper; he was fired. The Supreme Court held that Pickering's speech was protected by the First Amendment because it was of "public concern." Because *Pickering* so squarely rests on the "interests of the teacher, as a citizen, in commenting upon matters of public concern,"[405] it might appear inapplicable to in-class, taboo language by a school employee. Nonetheless, five federal appellate circuits apply *Pickering* to the in-class speech of teachers to exclude that speech from any First Amendment protection whatsoever.[406]

In these jurisdictions, teachers are stripped of any ability to use First Amendment academic freedom arguments to protect curricular decisions to use *fuck* in class.[407] Academic freedom is a concept used to defend a variety of speech and conduct activities. Academic freedom encompasses a professor's freedom to teach, freedom to research, and freedom to publish opinions on issues of public concern. Our notion of academic freedom is rooted in European traditions and in a general societal belief that education institutions are for the common good and their success hinges upon the "free search of truth and its free exposition."[408] The inability to use academic freedom as a defense to challenges to curricular decisions is a crippling blow to academia.

In contrast, five other circuits apply *Kuhlmeier* and require a reasonable relationship to a legitimate pedagogical concern before permitting schools to silence teacher curricular choice.[409] However, even before *Kuhlmeier* provided an alternative to *Pickering*, the First Circuit decided *Keefe v. Geanakos*[410] and recognized the academic freedom of high school teachers to make a curricular decision to use the word *fuck*. A senior English teacher assigned a reading from *Atlantic Monthly* that contained an "admittedly highly offensive... vulgar term for an incestuous son"—*motherfucker*. He was suspended, risked discharge, and sought injunctive relief, which was denied by the district court. The First Circuit reversed after conducting its own independent review of the article and finding it "scholarly, thoughtful and thought-provoking." Chief Judge Bailey Aldrich also included the following assessment:

> With regard to the word itself, we cannot think that it is unknown to many students in the last year of high school, and we might well take judicial notice of its use by young radicals and protesters from coast to coast. No doubt its use genuinely offends the parents of some of the students—therein, in part, lay its relevancy to the article.[411]

Chief Judge Aldrich recognized the value of studying *fuck* because of its taboo status.

The First Circuit revisited the issue again in *Mailloux v. Kiley*,[412] where another high school English teacher taught a lesson on taboo words that included writing *fuck* on the blackboard. Following a parent's complaint, he was fired for "conduct unbecoming a teacher."[413] At trial before the district court, Mailloux presented experts from both Harvard School of Education and MIT who testified as to the appropriateness of Mailloux's conduct. Additionally, the district court found that *fuck* was relevant to discussion of taboo words; eleventh graders had sufficient sophistication to treat the word from a serious educational viewpoint; and students were not disturbed, embarrassed, or offended. While the district court seemed to agree with the testifying experts that the way Mailloux used the word *fuck* was "appropriate and reasonable under the circumstances and served a serious educational purpose," divided opinion on the issue compelled the court to fashion a test for such situations. The district court crafted the following test:

> [W]hen a secondary school teacher uses a teaching method which he does not prove has the support of the preponderant opinion of the teaching profession… which he merely proves is relevant to his subject and students, is regarded by experts of significant standing as serving a serious educational purpose, and was used by him in good faith the state may suspend or discharge a teacher for using that method but it may not resort

to such drastic sanctions unless the state proves he was put on notice either by a regulation or otherwise that he should not use that method.[414]

Ultimately, the district court held that it was a violation of due process to discharge Mailloux because he did not know in advance that his curricular decision to teach about *fuck* would be an affront to school policies.

The First Circuit rejected the new test and the route taken by the district court, opting instead for a case-by-case analysis. Nonetheless, the panel affirmed the result because the teacher's conduct was within reasonable—although not universally accepted—standards and he acted in good faith and without notice that the school was not of the same view.[415]

RIGHT TEST, WRONG RESULTS

Despite these positive outcomes of reason over taboo, don't draw the wrong conclusion. Courts that apply the *Kuhlmeier* test to a teacher's in-class use of *fuck* might well come out the other way. In *Krizek v. Board of Education*,[416] the district court denied preliminary injunctive relief to an English teacher whose contract was not renewed after showing the movie *About Last Night* to her eleventh graders. The court described the film as containing "a great deal of vulgarity" including "swear words" and quoted the dialogue at length illustrating a liberal use of *fuckin'*, *fucking*, and *fuck*. The court considered and rejected the standards used in both *Mailloux* and *Keefe*. Then, applying the *Kuhlmeier* standard, the court found that the school had a legitimate concern over vulgarity and could find the film, with its frequent vulgarity, inappropriate for high school students. Consequently, the court rejected a preliminary injunction because the teacher was unlikely to prevail on the merits of her First Amendment claim.

Similarly, in *Vega v. Miller*,[417] the Second Circuit found that college administrators had qualified immunity from First Amendment claims by a college teacher who had been disciplined for permitting a classroom exercise, initiated for legitimate pedagogical purposes, to continue to the point where students were calling out a series of sexually explicit words and phrases.

The in-class exercise was a word association lesson known as "clustering" in which students select a topic, then call out words related to the topic, and finally group related words together into "clusters."[418] The students selected "sex" as the topic for the clustering exercise. Vega then invited the students to call out words or phrases related to the topic, and he wrote many of their responses on the blackboard including *clusterfuck*, *fist fucking*, and other taboo words.

To determine whether qualified immunity existed for the college administrators, the court explored what the clearly established rights were in this context. Although the court reserved the ultimate question of the constitutionality of the discipline, it had little difficulty concluding that no decision had clearly established that dismissal for Vega's conduct violated a teacher's First Amendment rights. Hence, qualified immunity was available to the college administrators.

Although these courts purport to use the same legal test for determining the First Amendment academic freedom of teachers, they reveal much inconsistency. An indirect use of *fuck* from a popular magazine is okay, but an indirect use of *fuck* from a popular film is not. Mailloux's English lesson using *fuck* as an example is protected while Vega's English lesson using *clusterfuck* is not. Eleventh graders need protection, but twelfth graders don't (but college students might). This is hardly the consistency we would hope for in constitutional speech protection.

If there is uncertainty in the application of the *Kuhlmeier* standard, the courts that apply the *Pickering* analysis don't fair much better as they strip educators of constitutional protection for in-class speech. For example, the Fifth Circuit used *Pickering* to reverse the district court's reinstatement of a university teaching assistant who spoke to an on-campus student group and referred to the Board of Regents as a "stupid bunch of motherfuckers" and said "how the system fucks over the student."[419] The district court had held that the Constitution protected her use of profanity because to prohibit particular words substantially increases the risk that ideas will also be suppressed in the process.

In reversing, the Fifth Circuit panel gave credence to the testimony of other English professors that "it shows lack of judgment to use four-letter words to any group of people" and that one who used such language was "ill fit for my profession." (With colleagues like that, the Board of Regents should be the least of your worries.)

This testimony, and the fact that it was credited by the court of appeals, is acquiescence to the power of taboo language. Not only do the English professors' comments, and the court's credence given to them, reflect the power of taboo, but the misapplication of *Pickering* may also be influenced by taboo. At least two critical questions seem to be answered the wrong way. First, the teacher was not in class but rather was outside of class when the comments were made. Second, she was commenting on topics not germane to her coursework, but of interest to the teacher, as a citizen, regarding matters of public concern. Literally punctuating taboo's influence, in the published opinion, the court refrained from printing the words *motherfucking* and *fucks* and used the asterisk euphemisms instead. Seems like the Fifth Circuit bungled this one at every turn.

In a more recent example of *Pickering* application, English professor John Bonnell openly and frequently used vulgar language in the classroom including *fuck*, *pussy*, and *cunt*.[420] After being accused of creating a hostile environment, Bonnell defended his use of language on the grounds that none of the terms were directed to a particular student and they were only used to make an academic point concerning chauvinistic degrading attitudes toward women as sexual objects. A female student ultimately filed a sexual harassment complaint based on his offensive comments; Bonnell responded by copying the complaint and distributing a redacted version to all of his students. This led to a disciplinary suspension for routinely using vulgar and obscene language, disruption of the educational process, and insubordination. Bonnell sued and ultimately the district court granted his injunction.

The Sixth Circuit, however, reversed, finding that the classroom profanity was not germane to the subject matter taught and was therefore unprotected speech. "Plaintiff may have a constitutional right to use words such as 'pussy,' 'cunt,' and 'fuck,' but he does not have a constitutional right to use them in a classroom setting where they are not germane to the subject matter, and in contravention of College's harassment policy."[421] The court left open the possibility that in-class use of taboo language that is germane to the subject matter might be permissible.

One glimmer of hope comes from *Hardy v. Jefferson Community College*.[422] In *Hardy*, a Sixth Circuit panel affirmed the denial of a motion to dismiss a community college instructor's claim that he was dismissed for using *nigger* and *bitch* in the context of a class discussion on social deconstructivism and interpersonal communications. The opinion by Judge Ronald Gilman (the dissenter in the Marilyn Manson T-shirt case) speaks of "the robust tradition of academic freedom in our nation's post-secondary schools," "the essence of a teacher's role [being] to prepare students for their place in society as responsible citizens," and the "unique place in First Amendment jurisprudence" held by educational institutions. This strong language supporting free speech in the academic context, particularly at the postsecondary level, is encouraging.

UNCERTAINTY WITH FACULTY *FUCK*

What then does this survey of faculty *fuck* use show? First, the federal appellate courts are divided on how to treat teacher use of taboo words, with half of the circuits choosing the rule from *Kuhlmeier* and the other half applying older *Pickering*. This decision in itself directly charts the course of tolerance for the use of *fuck* because *Pickering* analysis would not provide protection for in-class use. While the courts using *Kuhlmeier* could extend First Amendment protection to teachers' curricular decisions to use *fuck*, as *Krizek* illustrates, that doesn't always occur.

Although others have tried to synthesize the judicial treatment of *fuck* used by teachers in the classroom, the results are unsatisfactory. For example, Professor Robert Richards, of the Pennsylvania Center for the First Amendment and Penn State University, contends that the key is whether the speech is germane to the subject matter. According to Richards, "if I was teaching a media law class I could use the word 'fuck' when discussing the *Cohen v. California* case... [i]t would be germane to the subject matter. However, if I used the term repeatedly in math class, that would not be germane."[423]

Unfortunately, "germaneness" doesn't explain why relevant techniques used for legitimate pedagogical purposes (and hence germane) as found in *Vega* were not protected. Similarly, trying to make sense of the treatment of faculty use of *fuck* can't be explained by direct and indirect uses of the word. Direct uses of *fuck* as in *Mailloux* are protected while indirect uses of *fuck* as in *Vega* and *Krizek* are not—exactly the opposite of what we would expect.

Word taboo, however, helps explain the vastly different treatment afforded teachers' in-class use of *fuck*. I see the influence of word taboo on the parents who often initiate the complaints. Administrators and school boards allow fear of the word *fuck* to serve as a litmus test for competent teaching. Even judges who are on the front line of First Amendment protection can succumb to word fetish over *fuck*. Collectively, their extreme emotional reactions to *fuck* and its variations lead to the second-guessing of the curricular decisions made by the teaching professional in the best position to design appropriate curriculum for the student audience—the teacher in that class. As Chief Justice Earl Warren put it over fifty years ago:

> To impose any straitjacket upon the intellectual leaders in our colleges and universities would imperil the future of our Nation... Scholarship cannot flourish in an atmosphere of suspicion and distrust. Teachers and students must always remain free to

inquire, to study and to evaluate, to gain new maturity and understanding; otherwise our civilization will stagnate and die.[424]

The chief justice's warning that freedom of the mind is vital to our civilization isn't limited to our educational institutions. If the government puts muzzles on our mouths, it fosters suspicion and distrust not only in our schools but in our homes and workplaces as well. Is restricting the use of *fuck* a step toward cultural stagnation? To answer this question, the final chapter looks to the future of *fuck*.

CHAPTER SIXTEEN

Fuck Forever

Fuck is certainly a resilient word, but will it remain so? Is it destined to be dethroned as the king of dirty words by another four-letter word waiting in the wings? Will saturation and overuse eventually dilute its offensiveness? Is *fuck*'s fate the same obscurity of its sixteenth-century synonyms *jape* and *sarde*?

There are already commentators who believe *fuck*'s heyday has passed—Richard Dooling for one. He believes, "[f]or centuries, *fuck* was the most objectionable word in the English language, but now *nigger* and *cunt* are probably tied for that distinction, and *fuck* has at long last stepped down."[425] There is some evidence for this position. The results of research undertaken jointly by the Advertising Standards Authority, British Broadcasting Corporation, Broadcasting Standards Commission, and the Independent

Television Commission into the severity of words ranked *fuck* in third place behind *motherfucker* (second) and *cunt* (first).[426] *Nigger*, however, ranked as only the fifth most severe word, although rising from its eleventh place finish in 1997. These results could be discounted as a difference in British sensibilities. The fact that *wanker*, *bastard*, *prick*, *bollocks*, *arsehole*, and *paki* wind out the top ten bad boys leads me to believe that geography matters.

But what of *cunt*? Is it the new ultimate taboo word? *Cunt* certainly has a powerful sting to it—a venom that comes from its primary use as a derogatory term. *Cunt*, like *fuck*, is largely used for its emotive meaning as opposed to its referential one. But whatever points *cunt* wins in our fictitious contest for number one taboo status, it loses on versatility. *Cunt* lacks the linguistic versatility of *fuck*. It's still used largely as a noun. (There's no verb usage of *cunt* for example.) It's the great flexibility of *fuck* that allows it to reign supreme over the arguably more offensive but less useful *cunt*. Moreover, any prediction that *cunt* will surpass *fuck* may already be severely weakened by some women who have claimed the word as their own as a term of acceptance and power.[427] *Fuck* remains the hands-down winner over *cunt*.

But if *fuck* is losing its power, why? There are two possibilities: saturation and sexual mores. The saturation effect is easy to understand. *Fuck* is simply overused. Linguist Ruth Wajnryb suggests that *fuck*'s power is on the way out due to saturation: "In other words, nowadays it takes more

FUCKs to achieve what one lone FUCK would have achieved ten years ago."[428] With its referential meaning ignored, even *fuck*'s emotional force is nearly depleted. The more people hear a taboo word, the weaker the taboo. The overuse of *fuck* is basically bleeding it dry of its power. Collectively, we're becoming numb from the constant barrage of *fucks* thrown in our faces.

A second factor potentially contributing to *fuck*'s fall is sexual attitudes. One reason the word is less taboo today is that the sexual activity to which it is linked is less taboo. During the twentieth and now twenty-first century, American attitudes about sex have changed rather dramatically. What was a dark veil of ignorance has given way to accurate information on such things as birth control, abortion, pregnancy, impotence, and venereal disease. Acts that weren't even mentioned, much less performed, are now commonplace. As the underlying sexual taboos lift, the taboo of *fuck* lessens as well.

Yet whatever pressures may be diluting *fuck*'s power, the events of the previous chapters convince me that *fuck* as taboo remains. There are too many Boomers, Suiters, Herds, and Robinsons being thrown in jail for merely saying *fuck*. There are too many self-appointed censors like Southwest Airlines and the PTC targeting my T-shirts and my TV. The five unelected czars of the FCC can still make up rules on what I can see and extort million-dollar fines from the stations that breach them. Too many students and teachers still have their speech chilled at school; our workforce experiences the same. When using *fuck* invites these calamities, I maintain *fuck* is still taboo.

FUCK IS TABOO

Fuck is taboo—deep-rooted and dark. For over half a millennium, we've suppressed it. If the psycholinguists are right, we've done so for good reason. *Fuck* embodies our entire culture's subconscious feelings about sex—about incest, being unclean, rape, sodomy, disease, Oedipal longings, and the like. The word shoulders an immense taboo burden.

Recognizing the role of taboo, it is easy to understand why there is still such a reaction to the word. Taboo explains the individual reactions to *fuck* of my student, the sheriff, and the judge I mentioned in the opening chapter. It explains the difficulty faced by scholars trying to understand the word, whether their discipline is lexicography, linguistics, psychology, law, or another social science. For my purposes, taboo is also the tool that helps me understand why the law acts and reacts to the word *fuck* as it does.

Viewed this way, Chief Justice Warren Burger's fear that the Supreme Court would collapse if Brother John Harlan uttered *fuck* in the courtroom is understandable (as is Justice Hugo Black's concern for offending his wife). The individual reaction of parents to spare their children from the inadvertent broadcast or the calculating teacher now has a point of reference. The fanaticism of Chairman Michael Powell and Congressman Doug Ose is really their own disguised fear.

As all these individual reactions are writ large, taboo is institutionalized. As we look at the areas where *fuck* and the law commonly intersect, our progress toward escaping "from the cruel and archaic psychic coercion of taboo"[429] appears limited. From a constitutional vantage point, the First Amendment accommodates vulgar *fuck* when core political speech is involved (although I wonder whether the justices would have as much patience for "Fuck the Court").

Absent that clarity, the law permits taboo to marginalize *fuck* as speech, such as when the FCC declares *fuck* per se sexual or applies profanity standards to it. The same process allows private employers and public schools to chill workplace and school speech as judicial uncertainty promotes aggressive speech restrictions as safe institutional havens—for taboo, that is.

When taboo becomes institutionalized through law, the effects of taboo are also institutionalized. With *fuck*, the taboo relates to sex. We already lack the language to talk about sex; the whole point of the taboo is to make it difficult to bring up the topic. Wajnryb notes that "any explicit reference to sexuality force selection of terms drawn from the gutter, the nursery, or the anatomy class, each unsatisfactory for the purpose."[430] Institutionalized taboo guarantees that we continue to keep future generations in the dark.

To diminish the taboo effect, the solution is not silence. Nor should offensive language be punished. We must recognize that words like *fuck* have a legitimate place in our daily lives.

To reach this point, you must conquer the power the word has over you. Author Allan Sherman describes his experience to conquer the power of *fuck*:

> I put in a fresh sheet of paper, looked around to make sure nobody was watching, then shut my own eyes tight and pecked out the letters on the typewriter—F-U-C-K. After a decent interval I opened my eyes and looked. A jolt of adrenaline shot through my stomach. I had shocked myself... I ripped the page out of the machine, crumpled it up, threw it in a [sic] ashtray and set fire to it. But I didn't feel better; I felt worse... I promised myself, I shall overcome. I put a fresh page in the typewriter. Starting at the top left corner I typed, single space: fuckfuckfuckfuckfuckfuckfuckfuckfuckfu ckfuckfuckfuckfuck... from top to bottom. All told, there were 504 *fucks* on a page. Somewhere around number 327 a strange thing happened: The word ceased to frighten me.[431]

Each of us must confront *fuck* to conquer taboo.

Scholars must take responsibility for eliminating ignorance about the psychological aspects of offensive speech and work to eliminate dualistic views of good words and bad words. Taboo language should be included in dictionaries, freely spoken and written in our schools and colleges, printed in our newspapers and magazines, and broadcast on radio and television.

It's a small word. It might even seem, at first blush, too inconsequential, "but the issue it presents is of no small constitutional significance."[432] The future of *fuck* is clear. If we continue to allow the state to pick and choose the words we can use and the context in which we can use them, freedom is a stake. "The *fuck* you don't say today will be the one you won't be allowed to say tomorrow."[433] Once that word is extinguished, gone are its literally hundreds of uses, hence hundreds of ideas. Comfortable with a culture that allows offensive speech to be silenced, what other words rub you the wrong way? Maybe it's the rhetoric of non-mainstream religions or fringe political groups that offends you. This language can be targeted and eradicated, too. Now you might think I'm an alarmist and that the First Amendment stands to prevent precisely what I foreshadow. But before you discount my fears, please remember: *Fuck* is being fucked in the shadow of the First Amendment. Neither a Commission nor a court nor a cop should have power over our ideas. To ensure freedom of the mind, *fuck* must be set free.

Acknowledgments

Well, fuck. Of all the sections of this book, I find this the most daunting. Perhaps because reflection underscores just how many people influenced this project that I have selfishly thought of as my own. Or maybe it's simply the fear that I will omit someone who is praiseworthy and yet pay tribute to others less deserving. As in all stages of this enterprise, I'll do my best and hope for rough justice.

Let me start with the obvious—those who actually did something to further *Fuck*'s journey from my laptop to the top of your lap. Six research assistants, former law students of mine, allowed me to exploit them during the summers of 2003–08. Wail Alkatany (Ohio State Moritz College of Law Class of '03) started the project as a post-graduate assistant and demonstrated to me that there was something to say on this subject. Brian Roberts (Moritz '06) performed spectacular research and synthesized volumes of both legal and nonlegal sources. Joseph Bahgat (Moritz '07) worked on the article that preceded this book and helped get it out the door. Roy Hacker (Emory School of Law Class of '09) contributed additional research that propelled the article into a book. Whitney Timms (Moritz '10) edited and helped fine-tune the manuscript. Finally, Erin Hopper (Moritz '10) edited the whole thing not once but three times, I believe, making valuable contributions that the reader will hopefully attribute to me. Collectively, I couldn't have done *Fuck* without them.

Continuing the obvious category would be the folks at Sourcebooks, Inc. who published this book; you have my sincere thanks. I'm chilled by the realization that within my lifetime, publishing this book would have been a criminal act. Publishing it today with this title still pushes an envelope that deserves pushing.

Winding out the obvious category are those who literally facilitated the development of this manuscript. My thanks to the *Cardozo Law Review* for recognizing the value of my scholarship and publishing my law review article, "Fuck," when more timid law journals balked. Very special thanks to Dr. Reinhold Aman for his generous permission to republish from his vanguard journal on offensive language, *Maledicta*.

I also acknowledge the following for permission to reprint previously published material:

- Excerpt from Timothy Jay, *Why We Curse* (2000) p. 165. With kind permission by John Benjamins Publishing Company, Amsterdam/Philadelphia, www.benjamins.com.

- Excerpt from *American Heritage Dictionary of the English Language* (4th ed. 2000) p. 709. Copyright 2006 by Houghton Mifflin Harcourt Publishing Company. Reproduced by permission from *The American Heritage Dictionary of the English Language, Fourth Edition.*

- Excerpts from Allen Walker Read, "An Obscenity Symbol", 9 *American Speech* 264 (1934). Copyright 1934 by the American Dialect Society. All rights reserved. Used by permission of the publisher, Duke University Press.

- Excerpt from Robin Lakoff, *Language and Woman's Place* (2004) p. 44. By permission of Oxford University Press, Inc.

- Excerpt from David L. Hudson, "Free Speech on Public Campuses: Sexual Harassment," Jan. 15, 2005, http://www.firstamendmentcenter.org/speech/pubcollege/topic.aspx?topic=sexual_harassment. With permission from First Amendment Center Online.

Just as the concept of this book sprung from my experiences teaching at The Ohio State Moritz College of Law, the Moritz community has nurtured it in tangible and intangible ways. Two law school deans, Nancy Rogers and Alan Michaels, provided institutional support. My colleagues have been empowering. Ed Lee and Marc Spindleman have both been constant sources of encouragement and motivation. When outsiders marginalized my scholarship, Ruth Colker, Doug Berman, and Debbie Merritt (along with her son Danny Merritt) had my back and publicly made the case for my work. Likewise, Peter Shane and Martha Chamallas have been there to voice support and encouragement when it was needed. Indeed, the faculty of Moritz overwhelmingly supported my promotion even in the face of controversy over this scholarship; I am grateful. As much as I recognize the support of my colleagues, it's my students at Moritz (and Emory) who enrich me. They've taught me more than I could ever hope to teach them.

Outside of the Moritz community, I've been lucky to garner the support of some smart, vocal people who have stood beside me amid criticism. I'm especially grateful to Ann Bartow, Paul Caron, Brad Feld, and Michael Jensen for their kudos. Each has been supportive when I really needed it.

Of course, my family has been behind me throughout this effort. I acknowledge my mother, Valentina Zacharias, and her husband, David, my brothers Carl Mark, Cameron Michael, and Curtis Martin, their partners, spouses, and children—collectively a family that has supported me in the best way possible—by leaving me alone.

There are eight men who I must recognize who had nothing really to do with this book, but much to do with me. George Phelps—wherever he may be—was my teacher in freshman English at the University of Texas; he was the first teacher I ever had who said *fuck* in class.

My friend Gary Floyd is an artist, singer, and songwriter who has not only provided the soundtrack for my life but also encouraged me by example not to shy away from the controversial.

Four lawyers have employed, taught, and mentored me both personally and professionally: Judge Fortunato P. "Pete" Benavides of the United States Court of Appeals for the Fifth Circuit; Chief Justice J. Woodfin "Woodie" Jones of the Texas Third Court of Appeals; Ralph I. Miller and T. Ray Guy, both litigation partners at Weil, Gotshal & Manges LLP. These gentlemen continue to influence my life in countless ways and deserve public acknowledgement and my gratitude.

The late Charles Alan Wright was my professor and mentor at the University of Texas School of Law. But for his support, I doubt I would be a member of the legal academy. He died the day I arrived in Columbus, Ohio, to begin my law professor career. I've not had the benefit of his wisdom and guidance as my career developed. I often wonder what he would say about my focus on the law of dirty words. The only hint I have comes from a letter he sent me when I was still in private practice. After describing the type of work I was doing, he responded: "I suppose that spending your time defending the constitutional rights of direct-mail marketers to peddle their cheap junk nationwide is at least a step better than defending pornographers. And I would certainly be all for you even if you were doing the latter." If asked about this book, I surmise he would have some similar comment on whether I was using my talents to their fullest potential, but I think he would still be "all for me."

I have no doubt that my late father, Carl William Fairman, would be all for me. We were more alike than different; it was this similarity that tended to push us apart. I know he would like this book.

Finally, I have a very special thanks to Laura J. Fairman, who has not only put up with me for decades but also taught me nearly every meaning of the word.

This work is dedicated to our daughter, Mallory Claire Fairman, in the hopes that she will say it less and understand it more.

Endnotes

PROLOGUE

1. See, e.g., Catharine A. MacKinnon, *Toward a Feminist Theory of the State* 124 (1989) ("Man fucks woman; subject verb object."); Drucilla Cornell, "The Doubly-Prized World: Myth, Allegory and the Feminine," 75 *Cornell L. Rev.* 644, 690 (1990) ("But why is it the end of the world 'to be fucked?' Why do we think of all forms of oppression in terms of 'getting fucked?'").

2. See, e.g., Randall Kennedy, *Nigger: The Strange Career of a Troublesome Word* (2002); Jabari Asim, *The N Word* (2007).

3. See, e.g., Harry G. Frankfurt, *On Bullshit* (2005); Dominique LaPorte, *History of Shit* (Nadia Benabid & Rodolphe el-Khoury trans., 2002) (1978).

4. Email from editors of the *Harvard Law Review* to Christopher Fairman, professor of law (Mar. 8, 2006, 13:21:46 PST).

5. Email from articles editors of the *Kentucky Law Journal* to Christopher Fairman, professor of law (Apr. 17, 2006, 09:23:09).

6.   Using Westlaw, on July 15, 2008, I searched the *Harvard Law Review* database, HVLR, for the word *fuck*. The search produced thirty-three different articles using the word.

7.   Email from David Hague, Managing Editor, *Kansas Law Review,* to Christopher Fairman, professor of law (Apr. 11, 2006, 12:03:28).

8.   Camille Hébert, "Sexual Harassment is Gender Harassment," 43 *U. Kan. L. Rev.* 565, 585 (1995).

9.   Stephen R. McAllister, "Funeral Picketing Laws and Free Speech," 55 *U. Kan. L. Rev.* 575, 588 (2007).

10. Brian Leiter's Law School Reports (Apr. 13, 2006), http://leiterlawschool.typepad.com/leiter/2006/04/worlds_fastest_.html.

11. Discourse.net, http://www.discourse.net/archives/2006/04/this_is_pretty_funny.html (Apr. 13, 2006, 10:51 a.m.); Posting of Daniel J. Solove to Concurring Opinions, http://www.concurringopinions.com/archives/2006/04/rejected_in_a_h.html (Apr. 13, 2006, 3:35 p.m.).

12. bepress Legal Series: Most Popular Papers, http://law.bepress.com/expresso/eps/topdownloads.html (last updated Apr. 14, 2006) (listing "Fuck" as #1 most popular article based on the average number of full text downloads per day since the paper was posted).

13. Each month, the bepress Legal Repository team sends authors the monthly and aggregate downloads for each article or working paper posted to bepress. The download data comes from the monthly usage statistics issued May 2, 2006.

14. Dan Subotnik, "'Hands Off': Sex, Feminism, Affirmative Consent, and the Law of Foreplay," 16 *S. Cal. Rev. L. & Soc. Just.* 249, 265 n.98 (2007).

15. Using Westlaw, on July 21, 2008, I searched the *Southern California Review of Law and Social Justice* database, SCARLSJ, for the word *fuck*. The search produced seven different articles using the word.

16.   Posting of Ann Bartow to Feminist Law Professors, http://feministlawprofs.law.sc.edu/?p=416 (Apr. 13, 2006, 2:27 p.m.).

17.   TaxProf Blog, http://taxprof.typepad.com/taxprof_blog/2006/04/fairman_on_fuck.html (Apr. 15, 2006).

18.   Michael C. Jensen, "A Tenth Anniversary Message," Aug. 2007, www.ssrn.com (providing download data); SSRN Top 1500 Law Authors, www.ssrn.com (providing total all-time downloads per paper and new downloads [past twelve months] per paper for top 1,500 law authors) (last updated Feb. 14, 2009).

19.   Each week, SSRN publishes data on the SSRN Top Papers ranked by total new downloads available at www.ssrn.com. They also maintain an individual author site, in my case Christopher M. Fairman's Scholarly Papers, which has aggregate statistics and downloads per paper. The download statistics for "Fuck" were gleaned from the SSRN Top Papers download data for the relevant time period, my author page, http://papers.ssrn.com/sol3/cf_dev/AbsByAuth.cfm?per_id=343920 (last visited Feb. 20, 2009), the Abstract page for "Fuck," http://papers.ssrn.com/sol3/papers.cfm?abstract_id=896790 (last visited Feb. 20, 2009) (compiling Abstract views), and email from bepress Legal Repository to Christopher M. Fairman (Feb. 13, 2009, 09:44:05 PST).

20.   Most Downloaded Law Faculties, 2006, Leiter's Law School Rankings, Mar. 6, 2007. http://www.leiterrankings.com/faculty/2007faculty_downloads.shtml.

21.   Kennedy, supra note 2.

22.   Randall L. Kennedy, "'Nigger!' as a Problem in the Law," 2001 *U. Ill. L. Rev* 935 (2001).

23.   I am, of course, alluding to George Carlin's infamous "Filthy Words" monologue that was the basis of the Supreme Court's landmark

indecency ruling in *FCC v. Pacifica Foundation*, 438 U.S. 726 (1978). The seven words you couldn't say were *fuck, motherfucker, shit, piss, cunt, cocksucker*, and *tits*.

24. *Jacobellis v. Ohio*, 378 U.S. 184, 197 (1964) (Stewart, J., concurring) ("I know it when I see it.").

25. Britney Spears, "If U Seek Amy," on *Circus* (Jive Records 2009).

26. Jonathan Cohen, "Parents TV Council Protests Britney Song," Billboard.com, Jan. 21, 2009, http://www.billboard.com/bbcom/news/parents-tv-council-protests-britney-song-1003932995.story.

27. No one can download without first seeing the abstract page and seeing precisely what is offered. Bernard S. Black & Paul L. Caron, "Ranking Law Schools: Using SSRN to Measure Scholarly Performance," 81 *Ind. L.J.* 83, 122–23 (2006) (discussing SSRN safeguards).

28. Stefan Schmitt, "Fuck-Aufsatz: Der Jäger des F-Worts," Spiegel Online, Sept. 12, 2006, http://www.spiegel.de/wissenschaft/mensch/0,1518,436457,00.html (German-language article entitled "Fuck-Essay: The Hunter of the F-Word" about Fairman's article and research as well as the quest to find a publisher); Margaret Lyons, "5 Minutes with Christopher M. Fairman: 'Professor Fuck,'" *Time Out Chicago*, July 13, 2006, available at http://www.timeout.com/chicago/Details.do?page=1&xyurl=xyl://TOCWebArticles1 /72/out_there/5_minutes_with_christopher_m_fairman.xml.

CHAPTER ONE: WHY *FUCK*?

29. Allen Walker Read, "An Obscenity Symbol," 9 *American Speech* 264 (1934).

30. Leo Stone, "On the Principal Obscene Word of the English Language," 35 *Int'l J. of Psycho-Analysis* 30 (1954).

31. In re Schiff, Docket No. HP 22/92, Departmental Disciplinary Comm. for the First Judicial Department (N.Y. Sup. Ct. Feb. 2, 1993), sanction ordered, 190 A.D.2d 293 (N.Y. App. Div. 1993) in Stephen Gillers, *Regulation of Lawyers: Problems of Law and Ethics* 861 (6th ed. 2002).

32. Mich. Comp. Laws § 750.337 (2006).

33. *People v. Boomer*, 655 N.W.2d 255 (Mich. App. Ct. 2002); Steve Chapman, "Free Speech Rights Cover Even Those Naughty Words," *Chicago Tribune*, Apr. 7, 2002, at 9.

34. 465 U.S. 770 (1984).

35. Larry Flynt, *An Unseemly Man* 192 (1996). The case was *Keeton v. Hustler Magazine, Inc.*, 465 U.S. 770 (1984). Flynt tried to represent himself before the Supreme Court but was not allowed to do so, precipitating the outburst. When asked about the incident, Flynt said, "That was my finest hour." See Steve Benen, "A man with a triangulation plan," Salon.com, July 8, 2004, http://dir.salon.com/story/books/int/2004.07/08/flynt/print.html (interview with Larry Flynt). Flynt was certainly no stranger to courtroom antics. During the same Supreme Court incident, Flynt also wore a T-shirt under his dress shirt that said "FUCK THIS COURT." After his outburst, he was wheeled away by the bailiffs before he could expose it. Although the justices didn't get to see it, he did wear the shirt to his arraignment before a local D.C. judge later that day. According to Flynt, "The judge looked slightly amused but did not react to my shirt." Flynt, supra, at 227. There are conflicting accounts regarding the ultimate outcome of the contempt charge. Although Flynt says that the charges were dismissed, other reports disagree. Compare Flynt, supra at 227 ("In the end the charges were dismissed.") with Associated Press, "Larry Flynt Pleads Guilty," *New York Times*, Feb. 13, 1985, available at http://www.nytimes.com/1985/02/13/us/

larry-flynt-pleads-guilty.html?&pagewanted=print ("The publisher of *Hustler* magazine, Larry Flynt, has pleaded guilty in federal court to charges that he used threatening and abusive language before the United States Supreme Court.").

36.   Kevin Mayhood & Mark Niquette, "Expletive Lands Critic of Ruling in Court," *Columbus Dispatch*, Apr. 1, 2004, at 01C.

37.   Allan Sherman, *Rape of the A.P.E.* 22–23 (1973).

38.   Edward Sagarin, *The Anatomy of Dirty Words* 136 (1962).

CHAPTER TWO: UBIQUITOUS *FUCK*

39.   Eric Vanatta, "The F-Motion," 21 *Const. Comment.* 285, 288–89 (2004) (noting *fuck* had 24.9 million search engine hits compared to baseball, its closest competitor, with only 13.6 million hits).

40.   Despite attempts at censorship, *fuck* pops up on television. Robert S. Wachal, "Taboo or Not Taboo: That is the Question," 77 *Am. Speech* 195, 204 (2002) (identifying "What the fuck was that?" as an ad lib on *Saturday Night Live* [NBC television broadcast Apr. 12, 1997] and the use of *fuck* the next week to explain the prior accidental use); Jesse Sheidlower, Introduction to *The F-Word* xx, xxi (Jesse Sheidlower ed., 2d ed. 1999) (describing use on *Saturday Night Live* and Grammy Awards show). Of course, when *fuck* is broadcast over television today, the offending stations can be subject to FCC fines.

41.   Indrajit Samarajiva, "Fuck Linguistics: Use of Fuck on the Billboard Charts 1982–2002," Dec. 8, 2003, (unpublished manuscript), http://indi.ca/papers/fuckLinguistics.pdf (finding a significant increase in the use of *fuck* over the past twenty years in Billboard Top Ten Albums).

42.   Sagarin, supra note 38, at 136.

43. Patty Campbell, "The Pottymouth Paradox," *The Horn Book Magazine*, 311 May 1, 2007.

44. Jocelyn Noveck, "In Public, Expletive is Rarely Deleted Anymore," *Columbus Dispatch*, Mar. 29, 2006, available at http://dispatch.com/national-story.php?story=dispatch/2006/03/29/20060329-A1-04.html.

45. Posting of Benjamin Zimmer to Language Log, "Thinking specifically about the F-word," http://itre.cis.upenn.edu/~myl/languagelog/archives/002979.html (Apr. 2, 2006).

46. Barbara K. Kaye & Barry S. Sapolsky, "Offensive Language in Prime Time Television: Before and After Content Ratings," *J. of Broadcasting & Electronic Media* (Spring 2001).

47. "Oh, #@*¢!!," *Psychology Today*, May–June 1994, at 20, 21 (citing Timothy Jay's research).

48. Kaye & Sapolsky, supra note 46.

49. Timothy Jay, *Cursing in America*, 138, 157 (1992).

50. Andrea Millwood-Hargrave, "Delete Expletives?" 9 (2000), available at http://www.asa.org.uk/asa/research/archive/ (reporting results of research undertaken jointly by the Advertising Standards Authority, British Broadcasting Corporation, Broadcasting Standards Commission, and the Independent Television Commission).

51. "Lady Chatterley's Lover," *An Encyclopedia of Swearing*, 283 (2006).

52. *Grove Press, Inc. v. Christenberry*, 276 F.2d 433, 439 (2d Cir. 1960).

53. Id.

54. Sherman, supra note 37, at 19–27.

55. Helen Dewar & Dana Milbank, "Cheney Dismisses Critic with Obscenity," *Washington Post*, June 25, 2004, at A04.

56.   Amy Fagan, "Nation Inside Politics," *Washington Times*, June 28, 2004, at A05.

57.   Suzanne Moore, "Why Do Newspapers Use Asterisks? When Readers Read F*****g, I Imagine They Know What It F*****g Means," *New Statesman*, Aug. 16, 1999, at 14.

58.   Associated Press, "University Paper Takes Heat Over Obscenity," ABC News, Sept. 24, 2007, available at http://www.abcnews. go.com/print?id=3643546.

59.   Monte Whaley & Mike McPhee, "CSU editor admonished, will keep job," *The Denver Post*, Oct. 5, 2007, available at http://www. denverpost.com/search/ci_7081862.

60.   Internet Movie Database (IMDb), "Memorable Quotes for *Apocalypto* (2006)," http://www.imdb.com/title/tt0472043/quotes (last visited June 15, 2007).

61.   Fuck: Four Letter Film, About the Film, http://www.fourletterfilm. com/film.html (last visited Jan. 14, 2007).

62.   Id.

63.   French Connection, Brand Identity, http://www.frenchconnection. com/content/marketing/brand+identity.htm (last visited Apr. 13, 2009).

64.   "Fashion Firm Drops 'fcuk' Slogans," CNN.com, Oct. 3, 2005, http://www.cnn.com/2005/BUSINESS/10/03/fcuk.slogan/index. html; Posting of William Lozito to Strategic Name Development Product Naming Blog, "'FCUK' Goes Flaccid," http://www. namedevelopment.com/blog/archives/2005/10/fcuk_goes_flaccid. html (Oct. 5, 2005, 11:45 a.m.).

65.   Associated Press, "Barbra Streisand Tells Heckler to 'Shut the (Expletive) Up'," FoxNews.com, Oct. 10, 2006, http://www.foxnews. com/story/0,2933,219244,00.html; Associated Press, "Streisand has

outburst at NYC concert," *USA Today*, Oct. 10, 2006, available at http://www.usatoday.com/life/music/news/2006-10-10-streisand-outburst_x.htm; Brigitte Williams, "Vulgar Babs Rips Bush—and Fan—at MSG," *New York Post*, Oct. 10, 2006, available at http://www.nypost.com/seven/10102006/news/regionalnews/vulgar_babs_rips_bush___and_fan___at_msg_regionalnews_brigitte_williams.htm.

66. You too can watch it for yourself on YouTube at http://www.youtube.com/ watch?v=OnIu5CZNfDw. While you're at it, watch Jane Fonda say *cunt* one month later on the *Today Show* at http://www.youtube.com/ watch?v=o3qXUFyzrjM.

67. *Inside the Actor's Studio: Anthony Hopkins* (episode 1312) (Bravo television broadcast Oct. 15, 2007).

68. Internet Movie Database (IMDb), Memorable Quotes for *Inside the Actor's Studio* (1994), http://www.imdb.com/title/tt0169455/quotes. Lipton also recounts that when he asked David Chappelle for his favorite curse word, he said, "Fuck is my favorite. I say it a lot. You know, fuck. Yeah, I say it a lot." James Lipton, *Inside Inside* 433 (2007).

69. James Poniewozik, "How Bush Became the Curser in Chief," *Time*, June 7, 2007, available at http://www.time.com/time/printout/0,8816,1630538,00.html.

70. *Fox Television Stations, Inc. v. FCC*, 489 F.3d 444, 459-60 (2d Cir. 2006).

CHAPTER THREE: THE POWER OF TABOO

71. Stone, supra note 30, at 31.

72. Sanford Levinson, "The Pedagogy of the First Amendment: Why Teaching About Freedom of Speech Raises Unique (and Perhaps

Insurmountable) Problems for Conscientious Teachers and Their Students," 52 *UCLA L. Rev.* 1359, 1360, 1390 (2005).

73.   Timothy Jay, *Why We Curse* (2000) (developing the NPS or neurological, psychological, and social theory of cursing).

74.   Keith Allan & Kate Burridge, *Forbidden Words* (2006) (chapter 1 "Taboos and their origins").

75.   Lars Andersson & Peter Trudgill, *Bad Language* 55–56, 58 (1990).

76.   Allan & Burridge, supra note 74, at 4, 10.

77.   Valerie A. Curtis, "Dirt, Disgust and Disease: A Natural History of Hygiene," 61 *Journal Epidemial Community Health* 660 (2007).

78.   Richard Dooling, *Blue Streak* 43 (1996).

79.   Allan & Burridge, supra note 74, at 39.

80.   Dooling, supra note 78, at 42.

81.   Dooling, supra note 78, at 41 (citing Freud's *Taboo and Totem*).

CHAPTER FOUR: *FUCK* ETYMOLOGY

82.   Fred R. Shapiro, "The Politically Correct United States Supreme Court and the Motherfucking Texas Court of Criminal Appeals: Using Legal Databases to Trace the Origins of Words and Quotations," in *Language and the Law: Proceedings of a Conference* 367, 368 (Marlyn Robinson ed., 2003).

83.   "Fuck," *The F-Word* 117 (Jesse Sheidlower ed., 2d ed. 1999) (noting the initial citation as the poem attacking the Carmelite Friars of Ely and dating it as early as 1450–75).

84.   "Fuck," *American Heritage Dictionary of the English Language* 709 (4th ed. 2000) (Flen flyys translation).

85.   Id. (claiming *fuck* has been shocking from the first).

86. "Fuck," *An Encyclopedia of Swearing* 188 (2006) (claiming first recorded instance is Dunbar poem).

87. "In Secreit Place," in *The Poems of William Dunbar* 40 (James Kinsley ed. 1979).

88. Sheidlower, supra note 40, at xxv ("*Fuck* is a word of Germanic origin."); Dooling, supra note 78, at 32 (noting probable German origin).

89. Stone, supra note 30, at 42; James M. Ogier, "Sex and Violence in the Indo-European Languages," in 12 *Maledicta*, at 85, 86–88 (Reinhold Aman ed., 1996) (describing the relationship between *fuck* and *ficken* as spurious).

90. Read, supra note 29, at 267–68.

91. Stone, supra note 30, at 32.

92. William Whallon, "Wicked Cognates," in 12 *Maledicta*, at 25, 25 (Reinhold Aman ed., 1996) (explaining Indo-European etymology of *fuck* using Grimm's Law).

93. Eric Partridge, *Origins* 239 (1958) (noting the possible connection to *futuere* and *foutre*).

94. Sheidlower, supra note 40, at xxvi ("The relevance of structurally similar words in more distantly related languages [Latin *futuere*, for example], is unlikely."); Stone, supra note 30, at 42 (expressing doubts concerning the vowel change).

95. Read, supra note 29, at 268–69 (noting and criticizing Skinner for mistakenly tracing the word through the French).

96. Stone, supra note 30, at 42 (describing the combination of *foutre* and *ficken*).

97. "Fuck," *An Encyclopedia of Swearing* 188 (2006).

98. John T. Shipley, "The Origin of our Strongest Taboo-Word," in 1 *Maledicta*, at 23, 24 (Reinhold Aman ed., 1977).

99. Partridge, supra note 93, at 239.

100. Reinhold Aman, "Benedicta: An Editorial," in 1 *Maledicta*, at 1, 7 (Reinhold Aman ed., 1977) (describing curse); "Legal Curse," in 3 *Maledicta*, at 107 (Reinhold Aman ed., 1979) (hieroglyph for the curse).

101. Stone, supra note 30, at 31.

102. Read, supra note 29, at 268–74 (detailing the absence of *fuck* from dictionaries).

103. Stone, supra note 30, at 31 ("[T]he attack on obscene words in literature began even in Elizabethan times, and apparently increased in severity thereafter."); Read, supra note 29, at 269 (describing the strong current against use of low terms that started in the Elizabethan period and how the "hold of speech taboo became firmer" in the eighteenth century).

104. Read, supra note 29, at 271.

105. Id. at 272–74.

106. 6 *Oxford English Dictionary* 237 (2d ed. 1989).

107. Sheidlower, supra note 40, at xxi–xxii (identifying first printed example of *fuck* in United States as 1926).

108. Shapiro, supra note 82, at 370.

109. Id. at 371.

110. The term initialism is also used to describe a word formed from the initial letters of other words. As I understand the difference, an initialism is an abbreviation for a name where each letter of the abbreviation is intended to be pronounced separately such as FCC, BBC, or CIA. An acronym forms a totally new word, such as NATO.

111. A more complete list of false acronyms include:

"Fornication Under Carnal/Cardinal Knowledge"

"Fornication Under [the] Control/Consent/Command of the King"

"Fornication Under the Christian King"

"False Use of Carnal Knowledge"

"Felonious Use of Carnal Knowledge"

"Felonious Unlawful Carnal Knowledge"

"Full-On Unlawful Carnal Knowledge"

"For Unlawful Carnal Knowledge"

"Found Under Carnal Knowledge"

"Forced Unlawful Carnal Knowledge" (referring to the crime of rape).

Barbara Mikkelson, "What the Fuck," Snopes.com: Etymology of Fuck, http://www.snopes.com/language/acronyms/fuck.asp (last updated July 8, 2007).

112. Id. (debunking false acronyms); Ruth Wajnryb, *Expletive Deleted* 54–55 (2005) (on the two abbreviations).

113. According to the authoritative lexicographical work, *The F-Word*, these are "backronyms."

114. Nicholas Howe, "Rewriting Initialisms: Folk Derivations and Linguistic Riddles," *Journal of American Folklore*, Apr.–June 1989, at 171, 179.

115. Stone, supra note 30, at 35 (summarizing the fate of the early synonyms of *fuck*).

CHAPTER FIVE: LINGUISTS, PSYCHOLINGUISTS, AND TABOO

116. See Rei R. Noguchi, "On the Historical Longevity of One Four-Letter Word: The Interplay of Phonology and Semantics," in *Maledicta* XII, at 29, 38–40 (1996) (explaining *fuck*'s longevity over its rivals based upon its phonological pattern CV(C)C).

117. *The F-Word,* supra note 83, at 117–33 (identifying fourteen different verb uses); at 105–12 (listing ten separate noun uses); at 105–12 (listing ten separate noun uses); at 116 (defining *fuck* the adjective as "describing, depicting, or involving copulation; pornographic; erotic.—used before a noun"); at 141 (showing use as interjection); at 168–70 (noting adjective use of *fucking*); at 171–72 (noting the adverbial use as "exceedingly; damned"). For the curious, *absofuckinglutely* is an adverb meaning absolutely; *zipless fuck* is a noun meaning an act of intercourse without an emotional connection. Id. at 1, 272.

118. See Alan Crozier, "Beyond the Metaphor: Cursing and Swearing in Ulster," in 10 *Maledicta* 115, 122–23 (1988–89). *Fuck*[2] as a distinct word also has various uses as a part of speech. It can be used as a noun as in "you're as lazy as fuck," as a verb as in "I'm fucked if I know," as an adjective as in "This engine's fucked," and as an adverb as in "You know fucking well what I mean." Id. at 123–24. See generally Quang Phuc Dong, "English sentences without overt grammatical subject," in *Studies Out in Left Field: Defamatory Essays Presented to James D. McCawley on the Occasion of His 33rd or 34th Birthday* 3–10. (Arnold M. Zwicky ed., 1971) (discussing *Fuck*[1] and *Fuck*[2]).

119. Read, supra note 29, at 264–67.

120. Stone, supra note 30, at 30, 32, 35.

121. Read, supra note 29, at 277.

122. Ariel Arango, *Dirty Words: Psychoanalytic Insights* 185 (1989).

123. Dooling, supra 78, at 46.

124. Arango, supra 122, at 157.

125. Steven Pinker, "Why We Curse," *The New Republic,* Oct. 6, 2007.

126. John Ridley Stroop, "Studies of Interference in Serial Verbal Reactions," 18 *J. of Experimental Psychology* 643 (1935).

127. Pinker, supra note 125 (explaining Stroop effect).

128. Donald G. MacKay & Marat V. Ahmetzanov, "Emotion, Memory, and Attention in the Taboo Stroop Paradigm," 16 *Psychological Science* 25 (2005).

129. Pinker, supra note 125.

130. Allan & Burridge, supra note 74, at 249.

CHAPTER SIX: *FUCK* FETISH

131. Allan & Burridge, supra note 74, at 31–33 (discussing the three "-phemisms").

132. Philip Thody, *Don't Do It: A Dictionary of the Forbidden* 10 (1997).

133. 403 U.S. 15 (1971).

134. Levinson, supra note 72, at 1384.

135. Shapiro, supra note 82.

136. Robert Bloomquist, "The F-Word: A Jurisprudential Taxonomy of American Morals (in a Nutshell)," 40 *Santa Clara L. Rev.* 65 (1999).

137. Read, supra note 29, at 274 (on inverted taboo).

138. *Today* (Thames television broadcast, Dec. 1, 1976). A partial transcript of the exchange between Grundy and the Pistols is provided. It is clear that the interviewer was the instigator.

    BILL GRUNDY: I'm told that the group have received £40,000 from a record company. Doesn't that seem... er... to be slightly opposed to their anti-materialistic view of life?

    SEX PISTOL (Matlock): No. The more the merrier.

    BG: Really?

    SP (Matlock): Oh yeah.

BG: Well, tell me more then.

SP (Jones): We've fuckin' spent it, ain't we?

* * *

In response to a question about Beethoven, Mozart, Bach, and Brahms:

SP (Rotten): Oh yes! They really turn us on.

SP (Jones): But they're dead!

BG: Well, suppose they turn other people on?

SP (Rotten): [Mumbled] That's just their tough shit.

BG: It's what?

SP (Rotten): Nothing. A rude word. Next question.

BG: No, no. What was the rude word?

SP (Rotten): Shit.

BG: Was it really? Good heavens. You frighten me to death.

When Grundy asks part of the fan entourage if they were enjoying themselves, one woman, Siouxsie Sioux, responded:

FAN (Sioux): I've always wanted to meet you.

BG: Did you really?

FAN (Sioux): Yeah.

BG: We'll meet afterwards, shall we?

[Laughter]

SP (Jones): You dirty sod. You dirty old man!

BG: Well, keep going, chief, keep going. [pause] Go on. You've got another five seconds. Say something outrageous.

SP (Jones): You dirty bastard!

BG: Go on, again.

SP (Jones): You dirty fucker!

BG: What a clever boy!

SP: What a fucking rotter.

[More laughter]

BG [Turning to face the camera]: Well, that's it for tonight. The other rocker Eammon, I'm saying nothing about him, will be back tomorrow. I'll be seeing you soon, I hope. I'm not seeing you [to the band] again. From me though, goodnight.

[Closing theme and credits]

At the time, the Sex Pistols were vocalist Johnny Rotten, bassist Glen Matlock (later replaced by Sid Vicious), guitarist Steve Jones, and drummer Paul Cook. It is interesting that the bulk of the swearing came from Steve Jones and not Rotten, the more infamous of the group. The best way to appreciate the incident is to watch it yourself via YouTube at http://www.youtube.com/watch?v=0knFHyDD150.

139. Allen Walker Read, "Introduction" to Edward Sagarin, *The Anatomy of Dirty Words* 9, 9–10 (1962).

140. Llewellyn J. Gibbons, "Digital Bowdlerizing: Removing the Naughty Bytes," 2005 *Mich. St. L. Rev.* 167, 168 (2005) (describing Bowdler); Wajnryb, supra note 112, at 185–86.

141. Todd Murphy, "Clothes Call," *Portland Tribune*, Oct. 7, 2005, available at http://www.portlandtribune.com/news/story.php?story_id=32068; Michelle O'Donnell, "Passengers Check Your T-Shirt Before Boarding," *New York Times*, Oct. 9, 2005, § 4, at 14.

142. Associated Press, "Southwest Airlines makes man change T-shirt," CNN.com, Oct. 5, 2007, http://www.cnn.com/2007/TRAVEL/10/05/airlines.dress.debate.ap/index.html?iref=mpstoryview.

143. "Flight canceled after pilot drops F-bombs," MSNBC.com, Apr. 7, 2007, http://www.msnbc.msn.com/id/17999127/from/ET.

144. Dicks, "No Fuckin' War," on *PEACE*? (R Radical Records, 1984).

145. Joe Salmons & Monica Macaulay, "Offensive Rock Band Names: A Linguistic Taxonomy," in 10 *Maledicta* 81, 82, 91 (1988–89).

146. See Thor Christensen, "Hot Corner," *Dallas Morning News*, June 16, 2005, at 12E (describing censorship of the song). The song was replaced by another version titled "Don't Mess with My Heart." Id.

147. Paul Cashmere, "Parents outraged by Britney Spears song," Dec. 5, 2008, http://undercover.cm.au/News-Story.aspx?id=7081 (quoting parent Leonie Barsenbach).

    But don't rush to give Britney the blame (or praise) for this play on words. In 1922, James Joyce's *Ulysses* contained the following stanzas by the Prison Gate Girls:

    If you see kay

    Tell him he may

    See you in tea

    Tell him from me.

    James Joyce, *Ulysses* 616 (1922).

148. Jonathan Cohen, "Parents TV Council Protests Britney Song," Billboard.com, Jan. 21, 2009, http://www.billboard.com/bbcom/news/parents-tv-council-protests-britney-song-1003932995.story.

149. Press Release, Parents Television Council, "PTC Cautions Parents and Radio Stations about Indecent Britney Spears Song," Jan. 21, 2009, http://parentstv.org/PTC/news/ release/2009/0121.asp.

CHAPTER SEVEN: *FUCK* JURISPRUDENCE

150. Dooling, supra note 78, at 54.

151. 315 U.S. 568 (1942). Additional factual background comes from the case as well. Id. at 569–72.

152. *Street v. New York*, 394 U.S. 576, 592 (1969) (reversing conviction where it was inconceivable that defendant's words might have moved listeners to retaliate because speech was not inherently inflammable); *Cohen v. California*, 403 U.S. 15, 20 (1971) (discarding fighting words doctrine because it was not personally directed in a provocative fashion).

153. *Brown v. Oklahoma*, 408 U.S. 914 (1972). According to Justice Rehnquist, "[d]uring a question and answer period [Brown] referred to some policemen as 'm- - - - - f- - - - - fascist pig cops.'" 408 U.S. at 911.

154. *Roth v. United States*, 354 U.S. 476 (1957).

155. 413 U.S. 15, 24 (1973).

156. 403 U.S. 15 (1971). Additional background came from the case. Id. at 16–17, 20–21, 23, 25–26.

157. 438 U.S. 726 (1978).

158. The Commission's statutory authority provided at that time that "[w]hoever utters any obscene, indecent, or profane language by means of radio communication shall be fined not more than $10,000 or imprisoned not more than two years, or both." 18 U.S.C. § 1464 (1976).

159. *Pacifica*, 438 U.S. at 739–40.

160. "Complaints Against Broadcast Licensees Regarding Their Airing of the 'Golden Globe Awards' Program, 19 F.C.C.R. 4975 (Mar. 18, 2004) [hereafter *Golden Globe II*].

161. *Illinois v. Human Rights Comm'n*, 534 N.E.2d 161, 170 (Ill. App. Ct. 1989) (finding *fuck* and *motherfucker* general expletives).

162. *Stewart v. Evans*, 275 F.3d 1126, 1131–34 (D.C. Cir. 2002).

163. According to Eugene Volokh, these zero-tolerance policies are not hypothetical. Employers are enacting such broad policies and suppressing speech. See Eugene Volokh, "What Speech Does "Hostile Work Environment" Harassment Law Restrict?," 85 *Geo. L.J.* 627, 642 (1997).

164. *Tinker v. Des Moines Indep. Cmty. Sch. Dist.*, 393 U.S. 503, 506 (1943).

165. Id. at 510–11.

166. *Bethel Sch. Dist. No. 403 v. Fraser*, 478 U.S. 675, 685 (1986).

167. Merle H. Weiner, "Dirty Words in the Classroom: Teaching the Limits of the First Amendment," 66 *Tenn. L. Rev.* 597, 625–267 (1999) (discussing the circuit split and identifying the Third, Fourth, Fifth, Ninth, and D.C. circuits as applying *Pickering*).

168. See id. at 626–27 (identifying the First, Second, Seventh, Eighth, and Tenth circuits as applying *Kuhlmeier*).

169. Steamboat Willie has the line in the movie. "Memorable Quotes from *Saving Private Ryan* (1998)," http://www.imdb.com/title/tt0120815/quotes.

170. Tom Hanks, aka Captain Miller, says: "We're not here to do the decent thing, we're here to follow fucking orders!" Internet Movie Database (IMDb), "Memorable Quotes from *Saving Private Ryan* (1998)," http://www.imdb.com/title/tt0120815/quotes.

171. Complaints Against Various Broad. Licensees Regarding Their Airing of the "Golden Globe Awards" Program, 19 F.C.C.R. 4975 (2004) [hereinafter *Golden Globe II*].

172. Internet Movie Database (IMDb), "Memorable Quotes from *Saving Private Ryan* (1998)," http://www.imdb.com/title/tt0120815/quotes ("Lt. Dewindt: Yeah, Brigadier General Amend, deputy commander, 101st. Some fucking genius had the great idea of welding a couple of steel plates onto our deck to keep the general safe from ground fire.").

173. *Stewart v. Evans*, 275 F.3d 1126 (D.C. Cir. 2002).

174. *Duke v. North Tex. St. Univ.*, 469 F.2d 829 (5th Cir. 1973).

175. 415 U.S. 130 (1974).

176. See Noveck, supra note 44 (describing the results of an Associated Press poll conducted in March 2006 finding that 64 percent of those surveyed used the word *fuck*).

CHAPTER EIGHT: THEM'S FIGHTING WORDS!

177. *Chaplinsky v. New Hampshire*, 315 U.S. 568, 572 (1942).

178. Id. at 469–74.

179. *Chaplinsky v. State*, 18 A.2d 754 (1942).

180. *Chaplinsky*, 315 U.S. at 272–74.

181. *Terminiello v. Chicago,* 337 U.S. 1, 4 (1949).

182. *Street v. New York*, 394 U.S. 576, 592 (1969) (reversing conviction where it was conceivable that defendant's words might have moved listeners to retaliate because speech was not inherently inflammable).

183. *Rosenfeld v. New Jersey*, 408 U.S. 901 (1972). Rehnquist's dissent stated that Rosenfeld used the adjective "M- - - - - f- - - - -" four times. Id. at 910 (Rehnquist, J., dissenting).

184. *Brown v. Oklahoma*, 408 U.S. 914 (1972). According to Justice Rehnquist, "[d]uring a question and answer period [Brown] referred to some policemen as 'm- - - - - f- - - - - fascist pig cops.'" 408 U.S. at 911.

185. *Hess v. Indiana*, 414 U.S. 105 (1973).

186. *Lewis v. City of New Orleans*, 415 U.S. 130 (1974). *Lewis* actually went up to the Court twice. It was initially summarily reversed at 408 U.S. 913 (1972). Justice Rehnquist wrote in dissent: "G- - d- - - m- - - - - f- - - - - police." 408 U.S. at 909.

187. 405 U.S. 518 (1972).

188. 415 U.S. at 135.

189. 482 U.S. 451 (1987).

190. Id. at 471–72.

191. Id. at 453 n.1.

192. The Dicks, *Dicks Hate the Police* (R Radical Records 1980).

193. *People v. Boomer*, 655 N.W.2d 255 (Mich. App. 2002).

194. *People v. Boomer*, 653 N.W.2d 406 (Mich. 2002).

195. *State v. Suiter*, No. 257832001, 2001 WL 1002069 (Idaho App. Sept. 4, 2001). The dissenting judge insisted that Suiter had uttered no more than "a dismissive expression of disapproval of what the detective had been saying—the vulgar equivalent of 'go jump in the lake'" for which no criminal sanction was warranted under the First Amendment.

196. *State v. Suiter*, 56 P.3d 775 (Idaho 2002).

197. *Lewis v. City of New Orleans* (*Lewis I*), 408 U.S. 913 (1972); *Lewis v. City of New Orleans* (*Lewis II*), 415 U.S. 130 (1974).

198. See Cindy Horswell, "It starts with an 'F' and ends in two arrests," *Houston Chron.*, Mar. 14, 2009, at B4 (detailing the fate of Abraham Urquizo, a visitor from Jamaica, New York).

199. Urquizo pleaded guilty to the misdemeanor and was sentenced to time served—the hours after his arrest before he entered his plea. See id.

200. The plight of Kristi Fridge is also reported in the *Houston Chronicle*. See id. Unlike Urquizo, she plans to have her day in court with a trial set for later in 2009.

201. "Police charge woman who shouted profanities at overflowing toilet," USA Today.com, Oct. 16, 2007, http://blogs.usatoday.com/ondeadline/2007/10/police-charge-w.html; "Judge: Woman Who Cursed Out Toilet Protected Under 1st Amendment," FoxNews.com, Dec. 14, 2007, http://209.157.64.200/focus/f-news/1939580/posts.

202. 82 P.2d 27 (Mont. 2003).

203. 259 F.3d 1077, 1078 (9th Cir. 2001).

204. Burton Caine, "The Trouble with "Fighting Words": Chaplinsky v. New Hampshire is a Threat to First Amendment Values and Should Be Overruled," 88 *Marq. L. Rev.* 441, 548–50 (2004).

CHAPTER NINE: OBSCENITY—THEY KNOW IT WHEN THEY SEE IT

205. Acts and Laws of Massachusetts Bay Colony (1726), Acts of 1711–1712, ch. 1, p. 218, cited in *Paris Adult Theatre I v. Slaton*, 413 U.S. 49, 104 (1973) (Brennan, J., dissenting).

206. *Commonwealth v. Sharpless*, 2 Serg. & Rawle 91, 92 (Penn. 1815). In this case, a man was convicted for exhibiting a lewd painting showing a man and woman "in an obscene, imprudent, and indecent posture."

207. *Regina v. Hicklin* (1868) L. R. 3 Q. B. 360, 8 Eng. Rul. Cas. 60.

208. Edward De Grazia, *Girls Lean Back Everywhere: The Law of Obscenity and the Assault on Genius* (1992).

209. Haywood Broun & Margaret Leech, *Anthony Comstock: Roundsman of the Lord* 148, 202–03, 209 (1927).

210. David M. Rabban, "The Free Speech League, the ACLU, and Changing Conceptions of Free Speech in American History," 45 *Stan. L. Rev.* 47, 53–57 (1992) (discussing Comstock).

211. *United States v. Kennerley*, 209 F. 119, 121 (S.D.N.Y. 1913).

212. *United States v. One Book Called "Ulysses,"* 5 F. Supp. 182, 184 (S.D.N.Y. 1933), aff'd, sub nom. *United States v. One Book Entitled Ulysses by James Joyce (Random House, Inc.)*, 72 F.2d 705 (2d Cir. 1934).

213. *United States v. One Book Entitled Ulysses by James Joyce (Random House, Inc.)*, 72 F.2d 705, 708 (2d Cir. 1934).

214. *Commonwealth v. Gordon*, 66 Pa. D. & C. 101 (Q.S. Philadelphia County 1949).

215. 354 U.S. 476 (1957).

216. *Roth*, 354 U.S. at 484, 487.

217. 378 U.S. 184 (1964).

218. Bob Woodward & Scott Armstrong, *The Brethren* 198 (1979).

219. *Jacobellis*, 378 U.S. at 188.

220. Id. at 197 (Stewart, J., concurring).

221. See H. Franklin Robbins, Jr. & Steven G. Mason, "The Law of Obscenity—or Absurdity?," 15 *St. Thomas L. Rev.* 517, 526–27 n.82 (2003) (collecting cases).

222. 413 U.S. 15, 24 (1973); Dooling, supra note 78, at 61 ("Because of the well-established 'prurient' requirement, foul language and profanity are almost never considered obscene...").

223. Similarly, state obscenity statutes have been challenged because use of the word *shit* fails to meet the prurient interest test. For example, an Alabama statute making it unlawful for any person "to display in public any bumper sticker, sign or writing which depicts obscene language descriptive of sexual or execratory activities," was

unconstitutional as applied to a truck driver's bumper sticker, which read, "How's My Driving? Call 1-800-EAT-SHIT!" See *Baker v. Glover*, 776 F. Supp. 1511 (M. D. Ala. 1991).

224. *Spears v. State*, 337 So.2d 977 (Fla. 1976).

225. *Columbus v. Fraley*, 41 Ohio St. 2d 173 (1975).

226. In re Welfare of S.L.J., 263 N.W.2d 412 (Minn. 1978).

227. *Diehl v. State*, 294 Md. 466 (1982).

228. *State v Spencer*, 611 P.2d 1147 (Or. 1980).

CHAPTER TEN: "FUCK THE DRAFT": OFFENSIVE AND VULGAR SPEECH

229. *FCC v. Pacifica Found.*, 438 U.S. 726, 747 n.25 (1978) (describing facts of *Cohen*).

230. *People v. Cohen*, 1 Cal. App.3d 94, 97 (Cal. App. 1969).

231. Id. at 103.

232. *Cohen v. California*, 403 U.S. 15, 26 (1971).

233. Id. at 27 (Blackmun, J., dissenting).

234. 336 U.S. 490, 498 (1949).

235. *Cohen*, 403 U.S. at 27 (Blackmun, J., dissenting); id. at 28 (White, J., dissenting).

236. Woodward & Armstrong, supra note 218, at 128–133.

237. Id. at 129.

238. Id.

239. Id. (recounting Nimmer's thought that he would lose if he didn't say *fuck* at least once); Levinson, supra note 72, at 1365–66 (explaining that making the concession would probably not have constituted malpractice).

240. Woodward & Armstrong, supra note 218, at 129–33; Levinson, supra note 72, at 1360–62.

241. Woodward & Armstrong, supra note 218, at 130.

242. Id. at 131.

243. Id.

244. Id. at 133.

245. Id.

246. *Cohen*, 403 U.S. at 15.

247. S. 56, 118th Sess. (S.C. 2009).

248. Id.

249. Graeme Moore, "Bill would outlaw saggy pants in SC," Jan. 16, 2009, http://www.carolinalive.com/news/news_story.aspx?id=247814.

250. "State legislator seeks to criminalize bad language and droopy pants," Jonathan Turley, http://jonathanturley.org/2009/01/24/state-legislator-seeks-to-criminalize-bad-language-and-droopy-pants/ (Jan. 24, 2009).

251. Posting of Ken to Popehat blog, "Fuck off Robert Ford," http://www.popehat.com/2009/01/15/fuck-off-robert-ford/ (Jan. 15, 2009).

252. Senator Robert Ford, South Carolina Legislature Online, Feb. 27, 2009, http://www.scstatehouse.gov/members/bios/0606818109.html.

CHAPTER ELEVEN: *PACIFICA,* A PIG IN THE PARLOR, AND POWELL

253. 438 U.S. 726 (1978).

254. Id. at 729–30.

255. Reinhold Aman, "George Carlin's Milwaukee Six," in 2 *Maledicta* 40, 40–41 (Reinhold Aman ed., 1978).

256. *Pacifica*, 438 U.S. at 729–30.

257. The Commission's statutory authority provided at that time that "[w]hoever utters any obscene, indecent, or profane language by means of radio communication shall be fined not more than $10,000 or imprisoned not more than two years, or both." 18 U.S.C. § 1464 (1976).

258. Levinson, supra note 72, at 1365.

259. *Pacifica*, 438 U.S at 739–40, 744.

260. Id. at 745–46, 748–49.

261. Id. at 750–51.

262. Id. at 762–67 (Brennan, J., dissenting). Justice Brennan wrote a dissent joined by Justice Marshall. Justice Stewart also dissented and was joined by Justices Brennan, White, and Marshall. Id. at 777 (Stewart, J., dissenting).

263. Id. at 770. This is certainly the parenting approach I have taken in raising my daughter with no cataclysmic effects.

264. Id. at 766 (citing a similar metaphor drawn by Justice Stevens in *Butler v. Michigan*, 352 U.S. 380, 383 [1957]).

265. Federal Communications Commission Policy Statement on Industry Guidance on the Commission's Case Law Interpreting 18 U.S.C. §1464 and Enforcement Policies Regarding Broadcast Indecency, 66 Fed. Reg. 21, 984 (2001), available at http://www.fcc.gov/Bureaus/Enforcement/Orders/2001/fcc01090.doc.

266. Clay Calvert, "The First Amendment, the Media, and the Culture Wars: Eight Important Lessons from 2004 About Speech, Censorship, Science and Public Policy," 41 *Cal. W. L. Rev.* 325, 347 (2005).

267. Id. at 332–33.

268. Broadcast Decency Enforcement Act of 2004: Hearing on H.R. 3717 Before the Senate Comm. on Commerce, Sci., and Transp., 108th

Cong. (2004) (statement of Michael K. Powell, Chairman, Federal Communications Commission), available at http://hraunfoss.fcc.gov/edocs_public/attachmatch /DOC-243802A2.pdf.

269. FCC Indecency Complaint Form, https://www.parentstv.org/ptc/action/sweeps/main.asp (last visited Feb. 10, 2006) (allowing instant complaints to be filed against episodes of *NCIS* [CBS television broadcast Oct. 25, 2005], *Family Guy* [FOX television broadcast Nov. 6, 2005] and/or The Vibe Awards [UPN television broadcast Nov. 15, 2005]).

270. Calvert, supra note 266, at 330.

271. The song was "The Hands That Built America." The film was *Gangs of New York* (Miramax Films 2002).

272. Susan Crabtree, "FCC: You say it, you pay," *Daily Variety*, Jan. 14, 2004, at 66, http://www.variety.com/article/VR1117898480.html?categoryid=1064&cs=1(quoting Bono); Jim Rutenberg, "Few Viewers Object as Unbleeped Words Spread on Network TV," *New York Times*, Jan. 25, 2003, at B7.

273. Complaints Against Various Broad. Licensees Regarding Their Airing of the "Golden Globe Awards" Program, 18 F.C.C.R. 19,859 (2003) [hereinafter *Golden Globe I*] (memorandum opinion and order).

274. Clay Calvert, "Bono, The Culture Wars, and a Profane Decision: The FCC's Reversal of Course on Indecency Determinations and its New Path on Profanity," 28 *Seattle U. L. Rev.* 61, 71 (2004) (describing personal correspondence between Powell and PTC President Brent Bozell).

275. See, e.g., Crabtree, supra note 272, at 8 (quoting Michael Powell: "'I personally believe that it is abhorrent to use profanity at a time when we are very likely to know that children are watching TV'... 'It is irresponsible for our programmers to continue to try to push the envelope on a reasonable set of policies that try to legitimately

balance the interests of the First Amendment with a need to protect our kids.'"); Levinson, supra note 72, at 1383 (according to Powell, "if the F-word isn't profane, I don't know what word in the English language is").

276. Complaints Against Various Broad. Licensees Regarding Their Airing of the "Golden Globe Awards" Program, 19 F.C.C.R. 4975 (2004) [hereinafter *Golden Globe II*].

277. Id. at 4978, ¶ 8.

278. Id. at 4978–80.

279. Id. at 4981–82.

280. Jay, supra note 73, at 191; Levinson, supra note 72, at 1389.

281. *Golden Globe II*, supra note 276, at 4981, ¶ 14; statement of Chairman Michael K. Powell, id. at 4988 (noting this was the first time the profanity section was applied to *fuck* and stating that "today's decision clearly departs from past precedent"); statement of Commissioner Kathleen Q. Abernathy, id. at 4989 ("Rather, 'profane language' has historically been interpreted in a legal sense to be blasphemy.").

282. *Tallman v. United States*, 465 F.2d 282, 286 (7th Cir. 1972) ("'Profane' is, of course, capable of an overbroad interpretation encompassing protected speech, but it is also construable as denoting certain of those personally reviling epithets naturally tending to provoke violent resentment or denoting language which under contemporary community standards is so grossly offensive to members of the public who actually hear it as to amount to a nuisance."). That the Commissioners were compelled to dig up this stale definition of *profane* based on nuisance and offer it as authority is nothing short of amazing.

283. *Golden Globe II*, supra note 276, at 4981 n.34, ¶ 13 (citing *Black's Law Dictionary* 1210 6th ed. 1990 definition of profane).

284. Professor Levinson kindly refers to the miscategorization of *fuck* as "profane" as a "mistake." Levinson, supra note 72, at 1389. Professor Calvert finds it symptomatic of our broader culture wars and political opportunism. Calvert, supra note 274, at 75–85.

285. Michael Botein, "FCC's Crackdown on Broadcast Indecency," *N.Y.L.J.*, Sept. 13, 2005, at 4 (describing the FCC's penchant for piling one inference upon another to imply indecency). With profanity in particular, there is also the danger that the category will sweep more broadly than indecency given its link to vague terms such as "vulgar" and "coarse." Calvert, supra note 274 at 87.

CHAPTER TWELVE: PROFANITY, *PRIVATE RYAN*, AND A PRADA PURSE

286. *Saving Private Ryan* (DreamWorks SKG, Paramount Pictures Corp., & Amblin Entertainment, Inc. 1998).

287. Complaints Against Various Television Licensees Regarding Their Broad. on November 11, 2004, of the ABC Television Network's Presentation of the Film *Saving Private Ryan*, 20 F.C.C.R. 4507, at 4507-09 (Feb. 28, 2005) [hereinafter *Saving Private Ryan*].

288. Id. at 4507–10.

289. Id. at 4514, ¶ 18.

290. Botein, supra note 285, at 4.

291. The FCC received only 111 total indecency complaints in 2000 and a slightly higher 346 complaints in 2001. Then there was a dramatic upsurge in 2002 (13,922), 2003 (202,032), and in 2004 an amazing 1,068,802 complaints. Calvert, supra note 266, at 329.

292. Calvert, supra note 274, at 65 ("Broadcasters also may be more willing to rapidly settle disputes with the FCC over alleged instances

of indecent broadcasts rather than contest and fight the charges in the name of the First Amendment's protection of free speech."); Calvert, supra note 266, at 352–53 (describing Viacom's capitulation to a $3.5 million consent decree rather than fight the dispute for free speech).

293. Julie Hilden, "Four Major Television Networks Challenge the FCC's Regulation of Indecency: Why Modern Technology Has Made this Always-Dicey Area of Law Obsolete," FindLaw's Writ, Apr. 25, 2006, http://writ.news.findlaw.com/hilden/20060425.html (last visited May 5, 2006) (describing FCC's current fine policy as striking at the heart of free speech by putting content at risk).

294. As of December 31, 2005, Sirius reported it had exceeded its target subscriptions with 3.3 million, up from 1.1 million at the end of 2004. "Sirius Cash: Lots of Stock for Shock Jock," *Newsday*, Jan. 5, 2006, at A13.

295. See Ryan Saghir, "Clear Channel outlines Sirius-XM merger concessions," Mar. 13, 2008, http://www.orbitcast.com/archives/clear-channel-outlines-siriusxm-merger-concessions.html.

296. See Broadcast Decency Enforcement Act of 2004: Hearing on H.R. 3717 Before the Senate Comm. on Commerce, Sci., and Transp., 108th Cong. (2004) (statement of Michael K. Powell, Chairman, Federal Communications Commission), available at http://hraunfoss.fcc.gov/edocs_public/attachmatch/DOC-243802A2.pdf (citing the coarseness of TV and radio creating public outrage thereby justifying "punishing those who peddle indecent broadcast programming").

297. Professor Lynn Schofield Clark contends, "It is becoming more common in everyday conversation." Don Aucoin, "Curses! 'The Big One' Once Taboo, The Ultimate Swear is Everywhere, and Losing its Power to Shock," *The Boston Globe*, Feb. 12, 2004, at B13 (quoting Clark). Other commentators on American culture agree. Lance

Morrow contends that it is possible for *fuck* to become permissible: "I think that might happen... Somehow the whole sociology of [fuck] has changed." Id. (quoting Morrow).

298. Infinity Radio License, Inc., 19 F.C.C.R. 5022, at 5026, ¶ 12 (2004).

299. U.S. Census Bureau, Statistical Abstract of the United States 737, tbl.1117 (2006), available at http://www.census.gov/compendia/statab.

300. Annual Assessment of the Status of Competition in the Market for the Delivery of Video Programming, Twelfth Annual Report, 21 F.C.C.R. 2503, ¶ 8; 2505, ¶ 12 (2006).

301. Robert Corn-Revere, "Can Broadcast Indecency Regulations Be Extended to Cable Television and Satellite Radio?," 30 *S. Ill. U. L.J.* 243, 262–63 (2006) (discussing the role of the V-chip and ratings system in undermining the FCC indecency regime).

302. Kaiser Family Foundation, "Generation M: Media in the Lives of 8-18-Year-Olds 77," app. 1 (2005), available at http://www.kff.org/entmedia/7251.cfm.

303. It is interesting that Ose only objects to the language when used in free broadcast media. "When I'm subscribing to cable, I get it, OK. But when I watch free broadcast TV, me and my kids should not have to hear it." Crabtree, supra note 272 (quoting Ose). Ose is now a former congressman; he did not run for reelection in 2004.

304. See H.R. 3687, 108th Cong. (2003) (defining profane to include: "'shit,' 'piss,' 'fuck,' 'cunt,' 'asshole,' and the phrases 'cock sucker,' 'mother fucker,' and 'ass hole,' compound use [including hyphenated compounds] of such words and phrases with each other or with other words or phrases, and other grammatical forms of such words and phrases [including verb, adjective, gerund, participle, and infinitive forms"]. The so-called Clean Airwaves Act died in Congress—a fitting end to this form of censorship.

305. John Garziglia & Micah Caldwell, "Warning: Not for the Kids," *Legal Times*, Apr. 11, 2005, at 54 (noting congressional support raising FCC fine to $500,000 per violation); Calvert, supra note 266, at 351–52 (listing self-censorship examples induced by fear of FCC fines).

306. Noveck, supra note 44.

307. Stephen Labaton, "TV Networks, With Few Friends in Power, Sue to Challenge F.C.C.'s Indecency Penalties," *New York Times*, Apr. 17, 2006, at C3.

308. Fox and CBS filed a joint petition in the United States Court of Appeals for the Second Circuit. ABC filed in the United States Court of Appeals for the D.C. Circuit, which was subsequently transferred and consolidated in the Second Circuit.

309. Complaints Regarding Various Television Broadcasts Between February 2, 2002 and March 8, 2005, FCC 06-166, 39 Communications Reg. (P & F) 1065 (Nov. 6, 2006). The order also addresses the 2002 Billboard Music Awards incident involving Cher's "fuck 'em" comment, finding a violation under similar analysis. In addition to the *Early Show* incident, the order also dismisses various *NYPD Blue* complaints for procedural irregularities.

310. See id. ¶¶ 69–73.

311. Id. (Statement of Commissioner Jonathan S. Adelstein Concurring in Part, Dissenting in Part.)

312. You can view the oral argument by going to CSpan.org and searching for "*Fox v. FCC*."

313. 489 F.3d 444 (2d Cir. 2007).

314. 489 F.3d at 461.

315. Id. at 463.

316. 521 U.S. 844 (1997).

317. Fox, 489 F.3d at 467 (Leval, J., dissenting).

318. *F.C.C. v. Fox Television Stations, Inc.*, 128 S.Ct. 1647 (Mar. 17, 2008).

319. Posting of Christopher Fairman to The UTube Blog, "Fairman critiques FCC v. FOX case today at Supreme Court over 'fleeting expletives,' aka the 'F-word'," http://theutubeblog.com/2008/11/04/fairman-critiques-fcc-v-fox-case-today-at-supreme-court-over-fleeting-expletives-aka-the-f-word/ (Nov. 4, 2008).

320. 129 S. Ct. 1800 (2009).

321. Id. at 1812-13 (internal citations omitted).

322. Id. at 1813.

323. Id. at 1814.

324. Another case that could provide a proper vehicle for addressing the constitutional issues is *CBS Corp. v. F.C.C.*, 535 F.3d 167 (3d Cir. 2008), judgment vacated 2009 WL 1174862 (U.S. May 04, 2009). This case involves the network's appeal of a forfeiture penalty of $550,000 stemming from the exposure of Janet Jackson's breast during the live broadcast of the Halftime Show of the National Football League's Super Bowl XXXVIII in 2004. While the image was exposed on camera for only nine-sixteenths of one second, the FCC found the broadcast of Jackson's breast was indecent. The Third Circuit reversed due to the agency's failure to supply a reasoned explanation for the shift in policy concerning fleeting images. The Supreme Court granted the FCC's petition for certiorari, summarily vacated the judgment and remanded the case back to the court of appeals to reconsider in light of its decision in *Fox*.

325. Id. at 1819 (internal citations omitted).

326. Id. at 1819-22 (Thomas, J., concurring).

CHAPTER THIRTEEN: GENDERSPEAK AND THE WORKPLACE

327. On genderspeak, see Diana K. Ivy & Phil Backlund, *Genderspeak: Personal Effectiveness in Gender Communication* (3rd ed. 2004); Suzette Haden Elgin, *Genderspeak: Men, Women and the Gentle Art of Verbal Self-Defense* (1993). Language and gender research is often referred to as "LGR" in linguistics literature. As feminist approaches to the study of law have greatly enriched our discipline, recent feminist approaches to LGR demonstrate the complexity of the language-gender relationship. Karyn Stapleton, "Gender and Swearing: A Community Practice," in *Women & Language*, at 22, 22 (Fall 2003).

328. Ivy & Backlund, supra note 327, at 184–86.

329. See Stapleton, supra note 327, at 22–23 (surveying linguistic literature and noting general belief that women swear less as well as more recent studies exploring "the complex and situation-specific nature of 'women-swearing'"); Jean-Marc Dewaele, "The Emotional Force of Swearwords and Taboo Words in the Speech of Multilinguals," 25 *J. Multilingual & Multicultural Dev.* 204, 206 (2004) (reporting research on "S-T words" [swearwords and taboo words] finding males and those under thirty-five used more taboo words); Robert A. Kearney, "The Coming Rise of Disparate Impact Theory," 110 *Penn St. L. Rev.* 69, 89–90 (2005) ("Men, in fact, simply may be more vulgar and profane than women. In all-male work environments, men often use sexual profanity as a means of emasculating each other. In other words, sexuality is the language of insult."); Ivy & Backlund, supra note 327, at 171 (summarizing research from 2000 showing that men in the study [college students] were more likely than women to use highly aggressive terms to refer to sexual intercourse).

330. Wayne J. Wilson, "Five Years and 121 Dirty Words Later," 5 *Maledicta* 243 (Reinhold Aman ed., 1981) at 244 (methodology), 252 tbl.1

(Frequency of Using Dirty Words Expressed in Percentages), 248 (conclusions).

331. Read, supra note 29, at 274.

332. Jay, supra note 73, at 165 ("Ultimately, cursing depends on both gender identity and power; males tend to have more power to curse in public than females.").

333. Robin Lakoff, *Language and Woman's Place* 44 (1975).

334. Judith Mattson Bean & Barbara Johnstone, "Gender, Identity, and 'Strong Language' in a Professional Woman's Talk," in *Language and Woman's Place: Text and Commentaries* 237–38 (Mary Bucholtz ed., 2004).

335. 42 U.S.C. § 2000e-2(a)(1) (2000).

336. 477 U.S. 57, 64–65 (1986).

337. *Harris v. Forklift Sys., Inc.*, 510 U.S. 17, 21 (1993) (citations omitted).

338. See Linda Kelly Hill, "The Feminist Misspeak of Sexual Harassment," 57 *Fla. L. Rev.* 133, 145–49 (2005).

339. Kearney, supra note 329, at 89–90 ("Though the evidence is anecdotal, the difference in the way men and women use language is hard to ignore. The legal consequence is also significant. If women are less likely than men to use profanity in the workplace [at least for the reason that they do not choose to use it as the language of insult], is it such a stretch to say that they are also more likely to be offended by it when they witness it?").

340. *Katz v. Dole*, 709 F.2d 251, 256 (4th Cir. 1983).

341. *Baskerville v. Culligan Int'l Co.*, 50 F.3d 428, 430 (7th Cir. 1995) (Posner, J.).

342. *Burns v. McGregor Elec. Indus., Inc.*, 989 F.2d 959, 964 (8th Cir. 1993) (finding obscene name-calling including *bitch*, *slut*, and *cunt* was based on gender); *Human Rights Comm'n*, 534 N.E.2d at 170

(finding *cunt*, *twat*, and *bitch* were gender-specific terms). But see *Galloway v. General Motors Serv. Parts Operations*, 78 F.3d 1164, 1167 (7th Cir. 1996) (finding repeated "sick bitch" comment not gender-related term).

343. Kingsley R. Browne, "Title VII as Censorship: Hostile-Environment Harassment and the First Amendment," 52 *Ohio St. L.J.* 481, 492–92 (1991) (noting the use of "gender-specific terms" and "general sexual terms").

344. *Hardin v. S.C. Johnson & Sons, Inc.*, 167 F.3d 340, 345 (7th Cir. 1999).

345. *Torres v. Pisano*, 116 F.3d 625, 632–33 (2d Cir. 1997).

346. *Spencer v. Commonwealth Edison Co.*, No. 97 C 7718, 1999 WL 14486, at *8–9 (N.D. Ill. Jan. 6, 1999).

347. *Ptasnik v. City of Peoria*, 93 F. App'x 904, 908–09 (7th Cir. 2004) (failing to reach question of whether foul language and sexual comments were offensive when it was not directed at plaintiff but other women). But see *Torres*, 116 F.3d at 633 (noting that the fact that statements were not made in plaintiff's presence was of no matter because an employee who knows that her boss is saying things behind her back may reasonably find the working environment hostile).

348. *Angier v. Henderson*, No. Civ.00-215(DSD/JMM), 2001 WL 1629518, at *2 (D. Minn. Aug. 3, 2001) (*fuck, shit*, and *asshole* are gender-neutral profanity); *Human Rights Comm'n*, 534 N.E.2d at 170 (finding *fuck* and *motherfucker* general expletives); cf. *Rose v. Son's Quality Food Co.*, No. AMD 04-3422, 2006 WL 173690, at *4 (D. Md. Jan. 25, 2006) (*motherfucker* and "fuck her up" were not racially hostile).

349. *Ferraro v. Kellwood*, No. 03 Civ. 8492(SAS), 2004 WL 2646619, at *10 (S.D.N.Y. Nov. 18, 2004) ("fucking idiot" and "stupid

motherfucker" are neutral and nondiscriminatory); *Naughton v. Sears, Roebuck & Co.*, No. 02 C 4761, 2003 WL 360085, at *7 (N.D. Ill. Feb. 18, 2003) (citing *Hardin*, 167 F.3d at 345–46, as holding that "dumb motherfucker" and "when the fuck are you going to get the product" were neutral verbal abuse).

350. *Hocevar v. Purdue Frederick Co.*, 223 F.3d 721, 736–37 (8th Cir. 2000) ("Offensive language was used to describe both men and women.").

351. *Steiner v. Showboat Operating Co.*, 25 F.3d 1459, 1464 (9th Cir. 1994); *Bradshaw v. Golden Road Motor Inn*, 885 F. Supp. 1370, 1380–81 (D. Nev. 1995) (stating "fucking bitch" was a gender-based insult).

352. 25 F.3d 1459, 1464 (9th Cir. 1994). As Judge Fletcher's anecdote implies, it is being called a *bitch*, *broad*, or *cunt* that is the actionable gender-specific language; *fuck* merely intensifies it.

353. See *Hardin*, 167 F.3d at 345–46 (identifying coarse language including "dumb motherfucker" and "when the fuck are you going to get the product" as not being inherently sexual comments).

354. *Alder v. Belcan Eng'g Servs., Inc.*, No. C-1-90-700, 1991 WL 494528 (S.D. Ohio Nov. 27, 1991) (comments, including *fuck*, were not of a sexual nature).

355. *Stewart v. Evans*, 275 F.3d 1126, 1131–34 (D.C. Cir. 2002).

356. *Gross v. Burggraf Constr. Co.*, 53 F.3d 1531, 1544–46 (10th Cir. 1995). The court also found the comments not gender specific. Id. at 1546. In contrast, a supervisor who repeatedly refers to an employee as a "dumb cunt" is making a sexual remark and is subject to a hostile environment claim. See *Torres*, 116 F.3d at 632.

357. *Johnson v. Hondo, Inc.*, 125 F.3d 408, 412 (7th Cir. 1997) ("Most unfortunately, expressions such as 'fuck me,' 'kiss my ass,' and 'suck my dick,' are commonplace in certain circles, and more often than

not, when these expressions are used [particularly when uttered by men speaking to other men], their use has no connection whatsoever with the sexual acts to which they make reference—even when they are accompanied, as they sometimes were here, with a crotch-grabbing gesture."); *Lack v. Wal-Mart Stores, Inc.*, 240 F.3d 255, 261 n.8 (4th Cir. 2001) (accord).

358. *Bradshaw*, 885 F. Supp. at 1381.

359. Id. at 1380–81.

360. *Ptasnik*, 93 F.App'x at 909.

361. *Spencer*, 1999 WL 14486, at *8–9 (noting that profanities and crudities were generally directed and not actionable).

362. *Baskerville*, 50 F.3d at 430.

363. *Oncale v. Sundowner Offshore Servs., Inc.*, 523 U.S. 75, 80 (1998).

364. *Steiner*, 25 F.3d at 1461.

365. Several legal academics make this point. Kingsley Browne contends that vagueness in Title VII law leads employers to adopt overbroad speech regulation in contravention of the First Amendment. See Kingsley R. Browne, "Zero Tolerance for the First Amendment: Title VII's Regulation of Employee Speech," 27 *Ohio N.U. L. Rev.* 563, 580–97 (2001). Debra Burke argues that employers can regulate work speech, but in the process end up censoring employer and employee viewpoints. See Debra D. Burke, "Workplace Harassment: A Proposal for a Bright Line Test Consistent with the First Amendment," 21 *Hofstra Lab. & Emp. L.J.* 591, 621 (2004). Eugene Volokh posits that some employers suppress any speech that might possibly be seen as harassment with zero-tolerance policies. Volokh, supra note 163, at 635–37, 642.

366. Browne, supra note 368, at 575 n.77 (collecting dozens of citations to law reviews as a "partial list of articles devoted specifically to the

First Amendment and workplace speech"); Burke, supra note 368, at
612 nn.142–43 (collecting authorities addressing First Amendment
violations with Title VII and those showing the lack thereof).

367. Professor Browne makes one suggestion on the future of hostile
environment theory that I can't let go without comment. He calls
for the use of heightened pleading requirements similar to those
in defamation cases where the precise defaming language must
be pleaded or risk dismissal. Conclusory allegations should be
insufficient. The rationale is to allow defendants to quickly and
cheaply extricate themselves from meritless litigation. See Browne,
supra note 346, at 545–46. This is a particularly bad idea—already
rejected by the Supreme Court in *Swierkiewicz v. Sorema, N.A.,*
534 U.S. 506 (2002). I have been roundly critical of the use of
heightened pleading whether it is judicially imposed, statutorily
mandated, and most recently as required under Federal Rule of
Civil Procedure 9(b). See generally Christopher M. Fairman,
"Heightened Pleading," 81 *Tex. L. Rev.* 551 (2002) (criticizing
judicially imposed heightened pleading in civil rights cases and
statutory heightened pleading under the PSLRA and Y2K Act);
Christopher M. Fairman, "An Invitation to the Rulemakers—Strike
Rule 9(b)," 38 *U.C. Davis L. Rev.* 281 (2004) (advocating an
end to Rule 9(b)). If you care to read more about the subject of
heightened pleading in the defamation context (or any other), see
Christopher M. Fairman, "The Myth of Notice Pleading," 45 *Ariz.
L. Rev.* 987 (2003).

368. Browne, supra note 343, at 510–31 (applying and rejecting First
Amendment doctrines as a basis for Title VII speech suppression
including labor speech, captive audience, time-place-manner
regulation, defamation, fighting words, obscenity, and privacy).

369. In 1991 Professor Browne wrote that indecency theory couldn't be

used to contain *fuck*. See id. at 528–29. Unfortunately, the recent maneuvers by the FCC certainly provide a doctrinal basis for restricting *fuck* by labeling it as per se sexual and patently offensive as they did in *Golden Globe II*. Of course, I don't think this is any wiser for sexual harassment than for broadcasting.

CHAPTER FOURTEEN: TINKER'S ARMBAND, BUT NOT COHEN'S COAT

370. *Tinker v. Des Moines Indep. Cmty. Sch. Dist.*, 393 U.S. 503, 506 (1969).

371. *Hazelwood Sch. Dist. v. Kuhlmeier*, 484 U.S. 260, 266 (1988) (quoting *Fraser*, 478 U.S. at 675, and *Tinker*, 393 U.S. at 506).

372. Credit goes to Chief Justice Burger, who credits Second Circuit Judge Jon Newman for this line. *Bethel Sch. Dist. No. 403 v. Fraser*, 478 U.S. 675, 682–83 (1986) (quoting *Thomas v. Bd. of Educ., Granville Cent. Sch. Dist.*, 607 F.2d 1043, 1057 (2d Cir. 1979) [Newman, J., concurring]).

373. Andrew D.M. Miller, "Balancing School Authority and Student Expression," 54 *Baylor L. Rev.* 623, 643–44 & n.149 (2002) (describing various taxonomies stemming from the trilogy).

374. In 1969 the Court in *Tinker* upheld the right of middle school students to wear black armbands in protest of the Vietnam War. 393 U.S. at 509–11.

375. In *Kuhlmeier*, the Court allowed the school to exercise editorial control over a school-sponsored student newspaper so long as the regulation was legitimately related to an educational concern. 484 U.S. at 273.

376. In *Fraser*, the Court upheld the right of the school to punish a student

for making an elaborate, graphic, explicit, sexual metaphor. 478 U.S. at 685.

377. Id. at 684–85.

378. Under *Miller*, obscenity requires (a) the average person, applying community standards, would find the work, taken as a whole, appeals to the prurient interest; (b) the work depicts or describes in a patently offensive way sexual conduct specifically defined by the applicable state law; and (c) whether the work, taken as a whole, lacks serious literary, artistic, political, or scientific value. 413 U.S. at 24 (1973).

379. This necessarily requires the finding that the material is patently offensive—that is, explicit, graphic, repeated, and shocking.

380. *Miller*, supra note 376, at 646–49 (discussing confusion and calling for more precise definitional categories in order to create a more workable and understandable framework).

381. *Boroff v. Van Wert City Bd. of Educ.*, 220 F.3d 465 (6th Cir. 2000).

382. Id. at 470–71.

383. Id. at 466–67 (some citations omitted).

384. *Boroff*, 220 F.3d at 472, 473–74 (Gilman, J., dissenting).

385. *Castorina v. Madison County Sch. Bd.*, 246 F.3d 536, 540 (6th Cir. 2001).

386. *Frederick v. Morse*, 439 F.3d 1114 (9th Cir. 2006), rev'd, 127 S. Ct. 722 (2006).

387. *Morse v. Frederick,* 127 S. Ct. 722 (2006).

388. The Supreme Court denied certiorari in *Boroff.* 532 U.S. 920 (2001).

389. *Broussard v. Sch. Bd. of Norfolk*, 801 F. Supp. 1526 (E.D. Va. 1992).

390. *Pyle v. S. Hadley Sch. Comm.*, 861 F. Supp. 157, 158 (D. Mass. 1994).

391. 308 F.3d 939 (9th Cir. 2002).

392. See id. at 941–46 (describing the facts).

393. Judge Graber's application of *Kuhlmeier* (which she labels as *Hazelwood*) can be found at 946–54.

394. See id. at 955–56.

395. Id. at 957.

396. Id. at 962–64 (discussing use of limited public forum analysis).

397. See *Cornelius v. NAACP Legal Defense and Educ. Fund, Inc.*, 473 U.S. 788, 802 (1985).

398. See *Kincaid v. Gibson*, 236 F.3d 342, 354 (6th Cir. 2001) (en banc).

399. Brown, 308 F.3d at 964.

CHAPTER FIFTEEN: *FUCK* IN TEACHER SPEAK

400. *Tinker*, 393 U.S. at 506 ("It can hardly be argued that either students or teachers shed their constitutional rights to freedom of speech or expression at the schoolhouse gate.").

401. Levinson, supra note 72, at 1381.

402. *Vega v. Miller*, 273 F.3d 460, 467 (2d Cir. 2001).

403. *Tinker v. Des Moines Indep. Cmty. Sch. Dist.*, 393 U.S. 503 (1969); *Bethel Sch. Dist. No. 403 v. Fraser*, 478 U.S. 675 (1986); *Hazelwood Sch. Dist. v. Kuhlmeier*, 484 U.S. 260 (1988).

404. 391 U.S. 563 (1968).

405. Id. at 568.

406. Weiner, supra note 167, at 625–27 (discussing the circuit split and identifying the Third, Fourth, Fifth, Ninth, and D.C. circuits as applying *Pickering*).

407. Professor Weiner makes a persuasive argument for a new legal standard to protect social studies teachers who use sexually explicit material in the context of government or legal system lessons. See id. at 675–83.

408. *Barnes v. Washington St. Cmty. Coll. Distr. No. 20*, 529 P.2d 1102, 1104 (Wash. 1975).

409. Weiner, supra note 167, at 626–27 (identifying the First, Second, Seventh, Eighth, and Tenth Circuits as applying *Kuhlmeier*).

410. 418 F.2d 359 (1st Cir. 1969).

411. See id. at 361.

412. 448 F.2d 1242 (1st Cir. 1971), aff'g 323 F. Supp. 1387 (D. Mass. 1971).

413. *Mailloux v. Kiley*, 323 F. Supp. 1387, 1389 (D. Mass. 1971).

414. Id. at 1393.

415. *Mailloux*, 448 F.2d at 1243.

416. 713 F. Supp. 1131 (N.D. Ill. 1989).

417. 273 F.3d 460 (2d Cir. 2001).

418. Id. at 462–63.

419. See *Duke v. N. Tex. St. Univ.*, 469 F.2d 829, 832, 836–38 (5th Cir. 1973).

420. *Bonnell v. Lorenzo*, 241 F.3d 800, 802–03 (6th Cir. 2001).

421. The court relied on *Hill v. Colorado*, 530 U.S. 703, 716 (2000) ("[T]he protection afforded to offensive messages does not always embrace offensive speech that is so intrusive that the unwilling audience cannot avoid it.") and *Martin v. Parrish*, 805 F.2d 583, 584–85 (5th Cir. 1995) (college professor's captive audience does not allow denigration of students with profanity such as *bullshit, hell, damn, goddamn,* and *sucks*).

422. 260 F.3d 671 (6th Cir. 2001).

423. David L. Hudson, "Free Speech on Public Campuses: Sexual Harassment," Jan. 15, 2005, http://www.firstamendmentcenter.org/speech/pubcollege/topic.aspx?topic=sexual_harassment (quoting Professor Richards).

424. *Sweezy v. New Hampshire,* 354 U.S. 234, 250 (1957).

CHAPTER SIXTEEN: *FUCK* FOREVER

425. Dooling, supra note 78, at 18.

426. Millwood-Hargrave, supra note 50, at 9.

427. Llewellyn Joseph Gibbons, "Semiotics of the Scandalous and the Immoral and the Disparaging: Section 2(A) Trademark Law After *Lawrence v. Texas,*" 9 *Marq. Intell. Prop. L. Rev.* 187, 221–22 (2005) (describing how some lesbians have embraced *cunt* as a term of acceptance and empowerment); Suzanne Moore, "Why Do Newspapers Use Asterisks? When Readers Read F*****g, I Imagine They Know What it F*****g Means," *New Statesman*, Aug. 16, 1999, at 14 (noting reclamation of *cunt* by women). See generally Inga Muscio, *Cunt: A Declaration of Independence* (2d ed. 2002).

428. Wajnryb, supra note 112, at 40.

429. Arango, supra note 122, at 193.

430. Wajnryb, supra note 112, at 48.

431. Sherman, supra note 37, at 26–27.

432. *Cohen*, 403 U.S. at 15.

433. Dooling, supra note 78, at 37.

Index

About the Author

Christopher M. Fairman is a professor of law at The Ohio State University Moritz College of Law in Columbus, Ohio. Widely published in legal academic journals, Professor Fairman is a national expert in civil procedure, legal ethics, and now *fuck*. While these areas may appear diverse, Professor Fairman's scholarly interests can be easily summed up: words matter.

He makes this point in his civil procedure writings on pleading practice where he criticizes the requirement that civil rights plaintiffs have to say more in their pleadings to stay in court than other litigants. See "Heightened Pleading," 81 *Tex. L. Rev.* 551 (2002); "The Myth of Notice Pleading," 45 *Ariz. L. Rev.* 987 (2003); "An Invitation to the Rulemakers—Strike Rule 9(b)," 38 *U.C. Davis L. Rev.* 281 (2004).

Words also matter in the rules that govern lawyer ethics. When our current ethical rules prove inadequate, Professor

Fairman advocates for new ones that make clear to lawyers, especially those new to the profession, that ethical concerns count. See "Ethics and Collaborative Lawyering: Why Put Old Hats on New Heads?," 18 *Ohio St. J. on Disp. Resol.* 505 (2003); "A Proposed Model Rule for Collaborative Law," 21 *Ohio St. J. on Disp. Resol.* 73 (2005); "Why We Still Need a Model Rule for Collaborative Law: A Reply to Professor Lande," 22 *Ohio St. J. on Disp. Resol.* 707 (2007).

The importance of protecting words—even the four-letter ones—is at the heart of Fairman's most recent work, *Fuck: Word Taboo and Protecting Our First Amendment Liberties*, which builds on his scholarship in taboo language found in his recent popular article, "Fuck," 28 *Cardozo Law Review* 1171 (2007).

As an honor graduate of the University of Texas at Austin and the University of Texas School of Law, a former high school history teacher, a practicing litigator, and now a legal academic, Professor Fairman is skilled at explaining why things are the way they are. He is a gifted teacher with awards and recognition at the high school, college, and university level. It is that role that he cherishes. When asked to describe himself, he responded, "I'm a teacher."

A Kansan by birth, Fairman grew up in Austin, Texas. While he has had stints in Houston and Dallas as well, Austin will always be his hometown. Despite these deep Texas roots, he now makes his home in another capital city, with a major research university, built on a river—Columbus, Ohio.